ACTIVE MIND MAINTENANCE

TOOLS AND TIPS FOR IMPROVING COGNITIVE THINKING

FUNCTIONAL HEALTH SERIES

SAM FURY

Copyright SF Nonfiction Books © 2023

www.SFNonfictionBooks.com

All Rights Reserved

No part of this document may be reproduced without written consent from the author.

WARNINGS AND DISCLAIMERS

The information in this publication is made public for reference only.

Neither the author, publisher, nor anyone else involved in the production of this publication is responsible for how the reader uses the information or the result of his/her actions.

Nothing presented is medical advice. Implement anything you learn at your own risk. If in doubt, please consult a medical professional.

CONTENTS

Introduction	vii
Basic Brain Anatomy and Function	1
Cognitive Changes Across the Lifespan	3
An Overview of Cognitive Diseases	7
Neuroplasticity and Cognitive Rehabilitation	13
Mental Health and Its Impact on Cognition	15
Chronic Conditions and Cognitive Health	19
Genetic Factors in Cognitive Health	24
Environmental Influences on Cognitive Function	26
Sleep and Cognitive Function	29
Nutrition and Cognitive Health	31
Physical Activity and Cognitive Health	35
Mental Stimulation and Cognitive Reserve	38
Stress and Cognition	45
Social Engagement and Cognitive Health	47
Memory Improvement Techniques	50
Speed Reading and Information Retention	53
Critical Thinking and Logical Reasoning	55
Creativity and Problem-Solving	58
Emotional Intelligence	70
Technology for Cognitive Enhancement	85
General Cognitive Health Plan	91
Conclusion	93
About Sam Fury	97
References	98

All books in the Functional Health Series are transcriptions of masterclasses from within our members area.

As a member, you will get full access to all these masterclasses in eBook and audio format and a whole lot more at no extra cost.

Get 30 days access for just $1!

www.functionalhealth.coach/members

INTRODUCTION

There's no doubt that cognitive function plays a crucial role in how we navigate our daily lives. It affects our ability to remember important details, make informed decisions, and connect with others on an emotional level. Understanding and optimizing our cognitive health is not only essential for personal growth but also for maintaining a high quality of life as we age. In this masterclass, we will delve into the fascinating realm of cognitive function, exploring its foundations, ways to enhance it through lifestyle choices, and specific techniques to improve key aspects such as memory, critical thinking, and emotional intelligence.

To begin our journey, it's important to grasp the foundations of cognitive health. We'll explore the brain's intricate workings and shed light on the fundamental concepts, providing you with a solid understanding of the biological basis of cognition.

Moving forward, we'll delve into the ways we can enhance our cognitive health through our daily choices and habits. Research has shown that lifestyle factors like diet, exercise, sleep, and stress management can significantly impact our cognitive function. We will explore how these elements intertwine with our brain's well-being, providing evidence-based strategies to help you optimize your cognitive potential.

This masterclass will also equip you with specific techniques to enhance various aspects of cognitive function. Whether you're looking to boost your memory, sharpen your critical thinking skills, or enhance your emotional intelligence, we've got you covered. We'll dive into practical exercises and strategies, rooted in scientific studies, that you can easily incorporate into your daily routine to see real improvements in these areas.

In addition to memory, critical thinking, and emotional intelligence, we'll also explore other essential cognitive functions such as creativity, problem-solving, and decision-making. You'll discover how to harness your brain's full potential to excel in both your personal and professional life.

Whether you're a student aiming to improve your academic performance, a professional seeking an edge in your career, or someone who simply wants to maintain cognitive vitality as you age, this masterclass will be your guide. Together, we'll embark on a journey to unlock the secrets of cognitive function and empower you with the knowledge and tools you need to thrive in an ever-changing world.

BASIC BRAIN ANATOMY AND FUNCTION

The human brain is an incredible organ that serves as the command center of our body. It's responsible for everything we think, feel, and do. Understanding its anatomy and basic neurological functions is essential to grasp how our brains work. Let's take a closer look at the different parts of the brain and their functions.

At its core, the brain can be divided into three main parts: the forebrain, midbrain, and hindbrain. The forebrain is the largest and most complex part, containing the cerebral cortex, which plays a critical role in higher-level thinking, decision-making, and conscious awareness. The midbrain is involved in various sensory and motor functions, while the hindbrain manages basic life functions like breathing, heart rate, and coordination.

Within the forebrain, the cerebral cortex is divided into four lobes: the frontal, parietal, temporal, and occipital lobes. Each of these lobes has specific responsibilities. For instance, the frontal lobe, located at the front of the brain, is in charge of executive functions, such as planning, problem-solving, and personality. The parietal lobe processes sensory information, helping us understand the world around us, while the temporal lobe is crucial for memory and language comprehension. Lastly, the occipital lobe is primarily responsible for visual processing.

Beneath the cerebral cortex lies structures like the thalamus and hypothalamus. The thalamus acts as a relay station, relaying sensory information to the appropriate areas of the cortex, helping us perceive our surroundings. Meanwhile, the hypothalamus regulates vital functions like hunger, thirst, body temperature, and hormone production, making it a key player in maintaining homeostasis.

Moving down to the hindbrain, we find the brainstem, which includes the medulla, pons, and midbrain. The medulla controls essential automatic functions like breathing and heart rate, making it a vital survival center. The pons helps relay messages between different parts of the brain and plays a role in sleep and facial muscle movements. The midbrain manages various sensory and motor functions, including eye movement and auditory processing.

Furthermore, the brain is a vast network of interconnected neurons, specialized cells that transmit information through electrical and chemical signals. These neurons communicate with each other through synapses, forming complex neural pathways that underlie our thoughts, emotions, and actions.

This was a very basic overview of brain anatomy and function, but it is enough to demonstrate this marvel of nature, where different regions and structures work together harmoniously to shape our thoughts, behaviors, and emotions.

COGNITIVE CHANGES ACROSS THE LIFESPAN

Our cognitive functions undergo a series of transformations as we age. These changes can be influenced by various factors, including brain development, genetics, and life experiences. In this section, we will explore how cognitive functions change during childhood development and in the elder years, drawing insights from scientific studies to better understand these processes.

Cognitive development during childhood is an incredible journey that helps children learn and understand the world around them. It involves the growth of their thinking abilities, problem-solving skills, and the way they process information. This development is influenced by a combination of genetic factors, brain maturation, and the environment in which a child grows up. Several studies have provided valuable insights into the stages and patterns of cognitive development in childhood.

During the early years of life, from birth to about two years old, children go through a stage called the "sensorimotor stage." This stage was described by psychologist Jean Piaget. It's all about babies exploring the world using their senses and developing basic motor skills. They learn things like how to grasp objects and that when they can't see something, it still exists. For example, when you hide a toy under a blanket, they start to realize that the toy is still there even if they can't see it. This stage helps them build a foundation for understanding the physical world.

As children move into the next stage, which is the "preoperational stage" (from about two to seven years old), their thinking becomes more symbolic. They begin to use language to represent objects and ideas. This is when they start asking lots of "why" questions and are curious about everything around them. However, their thinking at this stage can be a bit limited when it comes to logical reasoning. They might believe that taller glasses have more juice in them, even if the amount is the same, just because the glass is taller.

Around the ages of seven to eleven, children enter the "concrete operational stage." Now, they become better at logical thinking, but it's mostly focused on concrete, real-life situations. They can understand concepts like addition and subtraction and can solve problems with real objects in front of them. However, abstract or hypothetical thinking can still be a bit tricky.

These stages of cognitive development in childhood are like building blocks. Each stage lays the foundation for the next, and they all play an essential role in shaping a child's ability to learn and make sense of the world. It's important to remember that children develop at their own pace, and there can be individual differences. Some kids might progress through these stages faster or slower than others, and that's perfectly normal.

During adolescence and beyond, individuals enter the "formal operational stage," and their cognitive development continues to evolve in remarkable ways. During this phase, there are significant improvements in thinking abilities, problem-solving skills, and the way they process information.

Adolescence, often defined as the period from around 12 to 18 years of age, is a time of rapid cognitive growth. One of the key developments during this stage is the maturation of the prefrontal cortex, a part of the brain responsible for higher-order cognitive functions. This maturation allows adolescents to engage in more advanced thinking, including abstract reasoning and decision-making. Studies using brain imaging techniques have shown that the prefrontal cortex undergoes significant changes in structure and function during adolescence, contributing to improved cognitive abilities.

During adolescence, individuals also enhance their problem-solving skills and critical thinking. They become better at considering different perspectives and making decisions based on complex information. This cognitive growth is vital for preparing young adults to face the challenges of the real world, such as academic and career-related decisions.

As individuals transition from adolescence into adulthood, typically around the age of 18 and beyond, cognitive development continues to progress. Young adults further refine their ability to think critically and make informed choices. They become more proficient in planning for the future, setting goals, and taking responsibility for their actions. Cognitive flexibility, the capacity to adapt thinking to changing situations, also improves during this stage.

Moreover, the acquisition of knowledge and expertise becomes a significant focus in adulthood. Young adults often pursue higher education and career development, which further enhances their cognitive abilities. Studies have shown that continuing education and engaging in intellectually stimulating activities can have a positive impact on cognitive function in adulthood, helping individuals maintain and even enhance their cognitive skills.

Cognitive changes as individuals move into their elder years are a natural part of aging. These changes are a result of various factors, including biological processes and environmental influences. As people grow older, they often experience shifts in memory, processing speed, and other cognitive functions.

One of the most common cognitive changes in older adults is a decline in processing speed. This means that it might take them a bit longer to process and respond to information compared to when they were younger. Research has shown that this decline in processing speed is linked to changes in the brain's white matter, which is responsible for transmitting information between brain regions.

A decline in working memory can also occur. Working memory is like our mental sticky note, allowing us to hold and manipulate information temporarily. Older adults may find it more challenging to juggle multiple pieces of information at once. However, it's important to note that not everyone experiences a significant decline in working memory, and some older adults maintain this function quite well.

Episodic memory, which involves remembering specific events or experiences, can also show changes in elder years. Older adults may have difficulty recalling details of recent events or experiences. This is a normal part of aging, but it's not the same as more severe memory problems like dementia, which is a separate condition.

While these cognitive changes are common, not all older adults experience them to the same degree. Individual differences play a significant role. Some people maintain their cognitive abilities well into their elder years through activities like mental stimulation, regular physical exercise, and social engagement.

Moreover, cognitive changes in elder years are not necessarily a one-way street of decline. Some research suggests that certain cognitive skills, such as crystallized intelligence (accumulated knowledge and expertise), can continue to improve or remain stable as people age. This highlights the complexity of cognitive changes in later life and the need to consider both declines and strengths.

AN OVERVIEW OF COGNITIVE DISEASES

Cognitive diseases are conditions that affect the way our brains work and how we think, remember, and process information. These diseases can have a significant impact on a person's daily life, as they can affect their ability to perform everyday tasks, communicate with others, and maintain their independence. While there are many different cognitive diseases, each with its own unique characteristics and challenges, we'll provide you with an overview that helps you understand the common threads and key concepts that tie them together. By the end of this section, you'll have a better grasp of the broad spectrum of cognitive diseases and the importance of early detection and intervention in managing them effectively.

Let's start with Alzheimer's Disease, a devastating cognitive disorder which has garnered increasing attention due to its profound impact on individuals and their families.

The story of Alzheimer's Disease begins in the early 20th century with the pioneering work of Dr. Alois Alzheimer. In 1906, Dr. Alzheimer presented a case study involving a patient named Auguste Deter, whose severe memory loss, confusion, and behavioral changes led him to discover distinct brain abnormalities during her autopsy. These abnormalities included the presence of amyloid plaques and neurofibrillary tangles, now recognized as hallmarks of the disease. Dr. Alzheimer's groundbreaking findings laid the foundation for our understanding of this disorder.

Over the decades, extensive research has unveiled the intricate pathophysiology of Alzheimer's Disease. It is primarily characterized by the accumulation of beta-amyloid plaques, abnormal protein deposits in the brain, and tau protein-driven neurofibrillary tangles, which disrupt neuronal function and communication. As these pathological changes progress, they lead to the widespread loss of brain cells, particularly in regions crucial for memory and cognitive functions, such as the hippocampus and cortex. This progressive neurodegeneration is at the core of the disease's relentless advancement.

Alzheimer's Disease manifests gradually, typically beginning with subtle memory lapses and difficulty with familiar tasks. As the condition advances, individuals may experience more pronounced cognitive deficits, such as impaired reasoning, language difficulties, and altered behavior. Accurate diagnosis is essential for early intervention. Clinicians utilize a combination of medical history, cognitive assessments, and neuroimaging studies, often ruling out other potential causes of cognitive decline. Biomarker tests, including cerebrospinal fluid analysis and positron emission tomography (PET) scans, are increasingly utilized to enhance diagnostic accuracy.

While no cure for Alzheimer's Disease exists, several treatments and therapeutic approaches aim to alleviate symptoms and slow disease progression. Cholinesterase inhibitors, such as donepezil, rivastigmine, and galantamine, are commonly prescribed to enhance cognitive function by increasing available neurotransmitters in the brain. Additionally, memantine, an NMDA receptor antagonist, helps regulate glutamate levels to manage symptoms. Lifestyle modifications, including diet, exercise, and cognitive stimulation, can also contribute to improved quality of life for individuals with Alzheimer's Disease. Ongoing research focuses on the development of disease-modifying treatments, targeting the underlying pathogenic processes to halt or reverse the disease's course.

Now let's move onto Dementia, which is a diverse and challenging group of neurological disorders that affect millions of individuals worldwide. It encompasses various subtypes, each with its unique characteristics, causing cognitive decline and impacting daily functioning. We are going to delve into some common types of dementia, including Parkinson's Disease Dementia, Vascular Dementia, Frontotemporal Dementia, and Lewy Body Dementia.

Parkinson's Disease Dementia is a condition closely associated with Parkinson's Disease. The history of Parkinson's Disease dates back to 1817 when British physician Dr. James Parkinson first described the motor symptoms characteristic of this disorder. Parkinson's Disease Dementia itself gained recognition in the later part of the 19th century when researchers began to notice cognitive impairment in individuals with Parkinson's Disease. Parkinson's Disease Dementia is characterized by the presence of Lewy bodies, abnormal protein aggregates, in the brain, which disrupt neural function and contribute to cognitive decline.

Symptoms of Parkinson's Disease Dementia often include memory impairment, attention deficits, and problems with executive functions. Visual hallucinations and changes in mood and behavior are also common. Diagnosis typically involves a comprehensive assessment of both motor and cognitive symptoms, with neuroimaging helping to confirm the presence of Lewy body pathology. Current treatments for Parkinson's Disease Dementia focus on symptom management. Medications such as levodopa may help with motor symptoms, while cholinesterase inhibitors can address cognitive impairment and hallucinations.

Vascular Dementia is intricately linked to vascular health and blood flow to the brain. Its history dates back to the mid-19th century when it was first recognized as a distinct form of dementia. Vascular Dementia is characterized by impaired blood supply to the brain, often due to strokes or small vessel disease. This disrupted blood flow damages brain tissue, leading to cognitive decline. Symptoms of Vascular Dementia can vary depending on the location and extent of vascular damage but often include memory problems, difficulties with reasoning, and impaired judgment.

Diagnosing Vascular Dementia involves assessing cognitive decline alongside evidence of vascular brain injury through neuroimaging. Management of Vascular Dementia revolves around controlling risk factors like hypertension and diabetes, as well as addressing underlying causes such as stroke prevention. Cognitive rehabilitation, physical therapy, and medications to manage associated symptoms may also be part of the treatment plan.

Frontotemporal Dementia is a less common but highly impactful form of dementia that was first described in the early 20th century. It primarily affects the frontal and temporal lobes of the brain, leading to changes in behavior, personality, and language skills. Frontotemporal Dementia encompasses several subtypes, each with distinct characteristics. It is often misdiagnosed due to its unique presentation, and diagnosis relies on clinical assessments, neuroimaging, and sometimes genetic testing.

Currently, there are no specific treatments to cure Frontotemporal Dementia, but management strategies aim to alleviate symptoms and enhance the quality of life. Behavioral interventions and speech therapy can be valuable in addressing the emotional and communication challenges posed by Frontotemporal Dementia.

Lewy Body Dementia is a complex and often underdiagnosed form of dementia. It was first recognized as a distinct condition in the early 20th century by Dr. Friedrich H. Lewy, who identified abnormal protein deposits in the brain. Lewy Body Dementia encompasses two primary subtypes: Dementia with Lewy Bodies and Parkinson's Disease Dementia, which we discussed earlier.

Lewy Body Dementia presents with a combination of cognitive symptoms, motor dysfunction, and fluctuating alertness. Visual hallucinations and Parkinsonism are common features. Diagnosis can be challenging due to the overlap with other conditions like Parkinson's Disease Dementia and Alzheimer's Disease. Neuroimaging and clinical assessments play a crucial role in differentiation. Management of Lewy Body Dementia involves addressing both cognitive and motor symptoms, often with medications such as cholinesterase inhibitors and dopaminergic drugs. Symptom-based strategies aim to improve quality of life and functional independence for individuals with Lewy Body Dementia.

To finish, we will briefly explore some of the less common cognitive diseases and disorders, starting with Huntington's Disease.

Huntington's Disease is a rare genetic disorder with a devastating impact. It was first described by Dr. George Huntington in 1872.

Huntington's Disease is caused by a mutation in the HTT gene, leading to the accumulation of abnormal protein aggregates in the brain. This results in progressive motor dysfunction, psychiatric symptoms, and cognitive decline. Current research in Huntington's Disease focuses on understanding the genetic underpinnings, exploring potential therapies to slow down or halt the disease progression, and improving symptom management. Recent studies have identified promising experimental treatments, such as gene silencing techniques, that aim to target the root cause of Huntington's Disease.

Creutzfeldt-Jakob Disease belongs to a group of rare, degenerative brain disorders known as prion diseases. Creutzfeldt-Jakob Disease was first documented in the early 20th century. Unlike many other neurodegenerative diseases, Creutzfeldt-Jakob Disease is infectious and caused by misfolded proteins known as prions. These abnormal proteins trigger a cascade of events leading to rapid cognitive decline, muscle stiffness, and behavioral changes. Current research efforts are concentrated on understanding prion biology, early detection, and exploring potential therapeutic approaches. Recent studies have shed light on novel diagnostic techniques, including cerebrospinal fluid biomarkers, that may aid in the early identification of Creutzfeldt-Jakob Disease.

Korsakoff Syndrome is a less common cognitive disorder primarily associated with chronic alcohol misuse. It was named after the Russian neuropsychiatrist Sergei Korsakoff in the late 19th century. This condition results from a deficiency of thiamine (vitamin B1), which impairs brain function, particularly memory. Current research focuses on improving our understanding of the neurobiology of alcohol-related brain damage and developing effective interventions. Studies have shown the potential benefits of thiamine supplementation and cognitive rehabilitation in managing Korsakoff Syndrome.

Progressive Supranuclear Palsy is another rare neurodegenerative disorder which was first described in the early 1960s. It affects movement control, balance, and eye movements, often leading to falls and difficulty with visual coordination. Cognitive impairment is also a common feature, although it may not be as prominent as in some other neurodegenerative diseases. Research in Progressive Supranuclear Palsy aims to uncover the underlying mechanisms, develop diagnostic biomarkers, and explore potential treatments. Recent findings suggest that targeting specific pathological proteins, like tau, may hold promise for PSP therapy.

While Alzheimer's, Parkinson's Disease Dementia, Vascular Dementia, Frontotemporal Dementia, and Lewy Body Dementia are well-known cognitive diseases, these less common conditions bring their unique challenges. Ongoing research efforts are crucial for improving our understanding of these disorders, advancing diagnostic methods, and developing more effective treatments.

NEUROPLASTICITY AND COGNITIVE REHABILITATION

Neuroplasticity is a remarkable phenomenon of the brain's ability to adapt and change throughout our lives. It refers to the brain's capacity to reorganize itself by forming new neural connections, strengthening existing ones, and even pruning away unnecessary ones in response to learning, experience, or injury. This incredible capability plays a crucial role in our cognitive development, allowing us to acquire new skills, recover from cognitive diseases or injuries, and adapt to various life changes.

One of the most inspiring aspects of neuroplasticity is its potential to aid in the recovery from cognitive diseases or injuries. Numerous studies have shown that the brain can undergo substantial rewiring to compensate for damage caused by conditions like stroke, traumatic brain injury, or neurodegenerative diseases such as Alzheimer's. For example, research published in the journal "Stroke" in 2013 demonstrated that stroke survivors can experience significant improvements in their motor skills and overall cognitive function through intensive rehabilitation programs. These programs leverage the brain's ability to reorganize itself, encouraging the formation of new neural connections to bypass damaged areas and regain lost functions.

Moreover, cognitive rehabilitation is an essential field that harnesses the power of neuroplasticity to help individuals recover from cognitive deficits. For instance, individuals who have suffered a traumatic brain injury may experience difficulties with memory, attention, or problem-solving. Cognitive rehabilitation programs use various techniques and exercises to stimulate the brain's adaptive capabilities. These interventions encourage the brain to create new neural pathways or strengthen existing ones, effectively improving cognitive functions over time.

In the context of neurodegenerative diseases like Alzheimer's, recent studies have explored the potential of cognitive training and stimulation to slow down cognitive decline. Research published in the journal "Neurology" in 2017 suggested that engaging in mentally stimulating activities, such as puzzles and learning new skills, could help preserve cognitive function in individuals at risk for dementia. These activities stimulate neuroplasticity, enabling the brain to build alternative networks that compensate for the damage caused by the disease.

MENTAL HEALTH AND ITS IMPACT ON COGNITION

Mental health and cognition are deeply interconnected aspects of human well-being. Our mental health not only affects our emotions and thoughts but also plays a significant role in shaping our cognitive abilities. In this discussion, we will explore the impact of various mental health conditions, including depression, anxiety, ADHD, and bipolar disorder, on cognition. By understanding these connections, we can appreciate the importance of addressing mental health as a fundamental aspect of cognitive well-being.

Depression is a mental health condition that affects not only our emotions but also our cognitive abilities. When someone experiences depression, it can bring about several changes in how their brain works, which, in turn, impact their thinking and memory.

Research studies have shown that people with depression often struggle with concentration. They may find it hard to focus on tasks or remember important details. It's as if their mind is filled with a fog that makes it challenging to think clearly. This can affect their performance at work or school and make it difficult to complete everyday activities.

Another common cognitive challenge in depression is memory problems. People with depression may have trouble recalling recent events or remembering important dates and tasks. This can lead to frustration and anxiety, as they may feel like they're forgetting things they shouldn't.

Slower processing speed is another aspect of cognition affected by depression. It might take longer for someone with depression to understand and respond to information or make decisions. This can be frustrating and make daily tasks feel more demanding than usual.

Depression can also influence executive functions, which are mental skills that help with tasks like planning, organizing, and problem-solving. When these functions are affected, it can be tough to set goals, make decisions, or even carry out day-to-day activities efficiently.

Now, while depression can indeed have a significant impact on cognition, it's essential to remember that these cognitive difficulties are not permanent. Effective treatment for depression, such as therapy and medication, can help improve cognitive functioning. Studies have shown that as depression symptoms improve, so do cognitive abilities.

Anxiety is another mental health condition that affects the way we think and how our mind works. Research studies have shown that anxiety often leads to racing thoughts and excessive worry. It's like having a mind that won't quiet down, making it challenging to concentrate on the task at hand. These racing thoughts can jump from one worry to another, making it hard to stay focused.

People with anxiety may also struggle with difficulty in concentrating. They might find it tough to pay attention to details or follow a conversation. This can affect their work or school performance and may lead to feelings of frustration.

Additionally, anxiety can make a person feel overly alert and vigilant. This heightened state of alertness can lead to hypervigilance, where they are always on the lookout for potential threats. While this can be helpful in some situations, it can also be mentally exhausting and make it challenging to relax or concentrate on non-threatening tasks.

Anxiety can also affect memory. People with anxiety might have trouble remembering things like where they put their keys or what they were just talking about. This can lead to feelings of frustration and self-doubt.

Decision-making can also be impacted by anxiety. People with anxiety may struggle with making choices because they are constantly evaluating potential outcomes and worrying about making the wrong decision.

Therapy and, in some cases, medication can help manage anxiety symptoms and improve cognitive functioning.

Bipolar disorder is characterized by mood swings, including manic episodes of elevated mood and depressive episodes. These mood swings can have various effects on cognitive abilities.

During manic episodes, individuals may experience heightened creativity and increased energy. However, their thoughts can become disorganized and erratic. They might have racing thoughts and find it challenging to focus on a single task. This can lead to impulsivity and risky decision-making.

Depressive episodes, on the other hand, can lead to cognitive slowing, memory problems, and difficulty with decision-making. People with bipolar disorder may struggle with concentration, making it hard to complete tasks that require sustained focus.

Research studies have delved into the cognitive aspects of bipolar disorder, revealing that during manic episodes, there's often a boost in cognitive abilities like creativity and problem-solving. However, these enhancements can come with the downside of impulsivity and disorganized thinking.

During depressive episodes, cognitive deficits can be more apparent, affecting memory, attention, and decision-making. These cognitive challenges can hinder daily functioning and contribute to the overall burden of the disorder.

Managing bipolar disorder typically involves mood stabilization through medication and therapy. Mood stabilizers help regulate the extreme mood swings, which, in turn, can help improve cognitive functioning. Psychotherapy can also provide individuals with strategies to manage their cognitive challenges effectively.

ADHD (Attention-Deficit Hyperactivity Disorder) is a neurodevelopmental condition. People with ADHD often experience challenges in areas related to attention, impulse control, and hyperactivity, which, in turn, influence their cognitive abilities.

One of the key cognitive difficulties associated with ADHD is attention problems. Individuals with ADHD may find it challenging to focus on tasks that require sustained attention, such as schoolwork or work assignments. They may become easily distracted by their surroundings or by their own thoughts. This can make it harder to complete tasks efficiently and accurately.

Another aspect affected by ADHD is impulse control. People with ADHD may act on their impulses without thinking through the consequences. This impulsivity can affect decision-making and lead to errors in judgment.

Executive functions, which include skills like planning, organization, and working memory, are also commonly impacted by ADHD. Difficulties in executive functioning can make it challenging to manage time, set goals, and stay organized.

Hyperactivity is another hallmark of ADHD, particularly in children. While it may not directly affect cognition, it can indirectly impact cognitive performance by making it challenging to sit still and focus.

Research studies have shown that the brains of individuals with ADHD may function differently, with differences in the structure and activity of certain brain regions. These brain differences can contribute to the cognitive challenges experienced by those with ADHD.

Effective treatments for ADHD often include behavioral therapy and, in some cases, medication. Behavioral therapy can help individuals develop strategies to improve attention, impulse control, and executive functioning. Medication, such as stimulants or non-stimulants, can also help regulate brain activity and improve cognitive performance.

Mental health conditions can indeed have a significant impact on cognitive abilities. Recognizing these connections is crucial for providing individuals with the support and treatment they need to maintain optimal cognitive well-being.

CHRONIC CONDITIONS AND COGNITIVE HEALTH

Many factors can influence cognitive function, and one significant factor is chronic physical health conditions. Conditions like diabetes, heart disease, and hypertension, among others, have been studied extensively for their impact on cognitive health, so in in this section, we'll explore how these chronic conditions can affect cognitive function.

Diabetes is a chronic medical condition that affects how your body uses and regulates sugar (glucose), which is a primary source of energy. It is closely associated with high blood sugar levels, and when blood sugar levels are consistently too high, it can damage the blood vessels and nerves in the brain. This damage can lead to problems with cognitive functions like memory, thinking, and problem-solving. Think of it like this: just as too much sugar can damage your teeth, it can also damage your brain if it's not controlled.

Moreover, diabetes is known to increase the risk of conditions like Alzheimer's disease and vascular dementia. Alzheimer's disease is a type of dementia that affects memory and thinking, while vascular dementia is caused by problems with blood vessels in the brain. Diabetes contributes to the development of these conditions by affecting the blood vessels and increasing the chances of harmful brain changes.

Another way diabetes can impact cognitive function is through its connection to other health issues. For example, diabetes often goes hand in hand with conditions like high blood pressure and high cholesterol. These conditions can further harm the brain by reducing blood flow and causing damage to brain cells.

Research has shown that people with diabetes who manage their blood sugar levels well have a lower risk of cognitive problems. So, controlling blood sugar through medication, diet, and exercise is crucial for preserving cognitive function in individuals with diabetes.

Heart disease, also known as cardiovascular disease, refers to a group of conditions that affect the heart and blood vessels. These conditions can include problems like coronary artery disease, heart failure, and arrhythmias. Heart disease can have a profound impact on cognitive function, affecting how our brains work.

One way heart disease can impact cognitive function is through reduced blood flow to the brain. Your heart's job is to pump blood throughout your body, including your brain. When someone has heart disease, it can lead to a decrease in the amount of blood and oxygen reaching the brain. This reduced blood flow can result in cognitive problems, such as difficulties with memory, thinking, and decision-making.

Furthermore, heart disease often coexists with risk factors like high blood pressure and high cholesterol levels. These risk factors can damage blood vessels throughout the body, including those in the brain. Damaged blood vessels can contribute to the development of small strokes or microinfarcts in the brain. These tiny strokes can accumulate over time and lead to cognitive decline.

Studies have also shown a strong link between heart disease and an increased risk of cognitive impairment and dementia. People with heart disease may be more likely to develop conditions like Alzheimer's disease, which affects memory and thinking abilities. The exact reasons for this connection are still being researched, but it's believed that the impact of heart disease on blood vessels and inflammation may play a role.

Moreover, medications used to treat heart disease, such as statins and anticoagulants, have been studied for their potential impact on cognitive function. Some research suggests that these medications may have both positive and negative effects on cognition, and the interactions between heart disease, its treatments, and cognitive health are complex and require further investigation.

Managing heart disease through lifestyle changes, medication, and medical supervision is crucial not only for heart health but also for preserving cognitive function.

Hypertension, also known as high blood pressure, is a common medical condition where the force of blood against the walls of the arteries is consistently too high. It can cause blood vessels to become narrower and less flexible, which can reduce the flow of blood and oxygen to the brain. When the brain doesn't receive enough oxygen and nutrients, it can lead to cognitive problems, such as difficulties with memory, concentration, and decision-making.

Moreover, hypertension is a known risk factor for more serious conditions like stroke, which occurs when a blood vessel in the brain becomes blocked or bursts. Strokes can damage brain tissue, leading to cognitive impairments depending on the extent and location of the brain affected.

Research has also shown that long-term hypertension may contribute to the development of conditions like vascular dementia. Vascular dementia is a type of dementia that is caused by problems with blood vessels in the brain. Over time, the cumulative damage from high blood pressure can lead to cognitive decline and memory problems.

Controlling hypertension through medication and lifestyle changes can help preserve cognitive function. Lowering blood pressure to a healthier range may reduce the risk of cognitive impairment and slow down the cognitive decline associated with hypertension.

Obesity is a condition characterized by the excessive accumulation of body fat, often resulting in a higher than normal body weight, and can often lead to chronic low-level inflammation throughout the body, including the brain. This inflammation is thought to contribute to cognitive problems, such as difficulties with memory, attention, and decision-making.

Moreover, obesity is closely linked to other health issues like type 2 diabetes and high blood pressure, both of which can harm cognitive function.

Research has also shown that obesity may affect the structure and function of the brain itself. Studies have indicated that obese individuals may have changes in brain areas related to memory and learning. These changes can make it harder to process and retain information.

Furthermore, obesity is often associated with poor diet choices, which can lack essential nutrients for brain health. Diets high in unhealthy fats and sugars and low in fruits, vegetables, and whole grains can negatively impact cognitive function over time.

Losing weight through diet and exercise interventions may help improve cognitive function in obese individuals. This indicates that managing obesity and adopting a healthier lifestyle can have positive effects on cognitive health.

Although there are other chronic conditions that affect cognitive health, the last one we will discuss is sleep apnea.

Sleep apnea is a sleep disorder characterized by repeated interruptions in breathing during sleep. These interruptions, called apneas, can last for seconds to minutes and can happen many times throughout the night.

Apneas cause brief awakenings from deep sleep to resume normal breathing, even if you're not aware of these awakenings. This constant interruption of sleep can lead to sleep deprivation and poor sleep quality, which, over time, can result in cognitive problems such as difficulties with memory, concentration, and problem-solving.

Furthermore, sleep apnea can cause oxygen levels in the blood to drop during apneas and then rise rapidly when normal breathing resumes. These oxygen fluctuations can lead to oxidative stress, which can damage brain cells and impair cognitive function.

Research has also indicated that sleep apnea is associated with an increased risk of conditions like mild cognitive impairment and dementia. The exact mechanisms linking sleep apnea to these conditions are still being studied, but it is believed that the chronic sleep disruption and oxygen fluctuations play a role in damaging brain health.

In addition, excessive daytime sleepiness, a common symptom of sleep apnea, can impact cognitive function by making it harder to stay alert, focused, and productive during the day. This can affect your performance at work or in daily activities.

Managing sleep apnea through treatments like continuous positive airway pressure therapy, lifestyle changes, and positional therapy can help improve sleep quality and reduce the impact on cognitive function. Seeking medical advice for proper diagnosis and treatment is essential for individuals with sleep apnea.

GENETIC FACTORS IN COGNITIVE HEALTH

Genetic factors play a crucial role in determining our cognitive health, affecting our ability to think, remember, and learn. These factors not only influence our susceptibility to cognitive diseases like Alzheimer's and dementia but also hold the potential for cognitive enhancement. Understanding how genetics can impact cognitive health is essential for developing strategies to prevent cognitive decline and improve cognitive abilities.

Research has shown that genetics can significantly affect the risk of developing cognitive diseases like the ones previously mentioned. For instance, certain genes, like APOE ε4, have been identified as strong risk factors for Alzheimer's. People carrying one or two copies of this gene variant have a higher likelihood of developing the disease compared to those without it. Additionally, several other genetic variations have been associated with an increased risk of dementia and cognitive decline. These genetic factors can interact with environmental factors, making some individuals more vulnerable to cognitive diseases than others.

Understanding these genetic factors is essential for early detection and prevention. By identifying individuals with a higher genetic risk, healthcare professionals can provide personalized care and interventions to mitigate the impact of cognitive diseases.

Genetic tests are available that can provide information about your risk of developing cognitive diseases and can be obtained through your healthcare professional.

While genetics can influence our susceptibility to cognitive diseases, they also contribute to our cognitive abilities. Genetic variations can affect factors such as memory, attention, and problem-solving skills. Recent research has explored the idea of using genetics to enhance cognitive function. For instance, the discovery of certain gene variants associated with exceptional memory or cognitive resilience has raised the possibility of developing targeted interventions or therapies to enhance cognitive performance.

Moreover, genetic research has opened the door to personalized approaches for cognitive enhancement. By analyzing an individual's genetic profile, scientists can tailor interventions to optimize cognitive function. This may include lifestyle changes, dietary adjustments, or even pharmaceutical interventions designed specifically for an individual's genetic makeup.

However, it's important to note that the field of cognitive enhancement through genetics is still in its infancy, and ethical considerations and potential risks must be carefully addressed. Ensuring the responsible use of genetic information for cognitive enhancement is crucial to avoid unintended consequences.

ENVIRONMENTAL INFLUENCES ON COGNITIVE FUNCTION

Our ability to think, learn, and remember is not solely determined by our genetics; it can also be profoundly affected by the world around us. Let's explore how factors such as pollution, living conditions, and exposure to toxins can impact cognitive health.

Air pollution is a major environmental issue that affects not only our physical health but also our cognitive function. Firstly, it's essential to understand what air pollution is made up of. It contains tiny particles, known as fine particulate matter, and gases like nitrogen dioxide. These pollutants are released from vehicles, factories, and other sources and can find their way into the air we breathe.

When we breathe in polluted air, these tiny particles and gases can make their way into our bloodstream and even reach our brains. Research has shown that exposure to high levels of air pollution, especially over an extended period, can lead to cognitive problems. For instance, children exposed to higher levels of air pollution tend to perform worse on cognitive tests and may have developmental delays.

One study conducted in the United States found that people who lived in areas with higher levels of air pollution experienced a more rapid decline in cognitive function as they aged. This decline was particularly noticeable in memory and language skills. Another study in China found that exposure to air pollution was associated with a higher risk of developing Alzheimer's disease and other neurodegenerative conditions.

So, how does air pollution harm our cognitive function? It's thought that the pollutants in the air can cause inflammation in our brains. This inflammation can damage brain cells and disrupt the normal functioning of our neural networks, which are essential for thinking, learning, and memory.

Moreover, air pollution can affect blood flow to the brain. Research suggests that it may reduce the flow of oxygen and nutrients to brain cells, further impairing cognitive abilities. Additionally, the oxidative stress caused by pollutants can lead to the production of harmful molecules known as free radicals, which can damage brain cells and DNA.

The quality of one's living conditions can also have a significant impact on cognitive function. Overcrowded and noisy living environments can lead to stress, which can impair memory and attention. Noise pollution, such as loud traffic or construction sounds, can disrupt sleep patterns, which are essential for cognitive restoration and consolidation of memories.

Additionally, a study published in the journal "Psychological Science" found that cluttered environments can reduce the ability to process information effectively and make decisions.

Socioeconomic factors play a significant role in determining living conditions, and these factors can, in turn, impact cognitive function. People with limited access to educational resources and opportunities may have reduced cognitive abilities. For instance, children growing up in impoverished neighborhoods may have less access to quality educational programs, books, and stimulating activities, which are crucial for cognitive development. Numerous studies have highlighted the importance of early childhood education and access to enriching environments in promoting cognitive growth.

On the positive side, living in safe, clean, and supportive environments can have a beneficial impact on cognitive function. Access to parks and green spaces has been associated with improved cognitive development, particularly in children. Being surrounded by nature and having opportunities for physical activity can enhance attention, memory, and problem-solving skills.

Finally, exposure to toxins is a significant concern when it comes to cognitive function. Let's start with lead, a well-known toxic metal. Even at low levels of exposure, lead can be harmful, especially to the developing brains of children. Studies have shown that children exposed to lead may experience cognitive deficits, learning disabilities, and behavioral problems. Research has also indicated that lead exposure in childhood can have long-lasting effects, affecting cognitive function well into adulthood.

Mercury is another toxin that can negatively influence cognitive function. This toxin is often found in contaminated fish and seafood. When people consume mercury-contaminated foods, especially pregnant women and young children, it can harm the developing brain.

Exposure to toxins like lead and mercury interfere with the communication between brain cells, which is crucial for cognitive processes. They can also cause oxidative stress, leading to the production of harmful molecules called free radicals that damage brain cells and DNA.

One study published in the journal "Environmental Health Perspectives" found that even low levels of lead exposure were associated with cognitive decline in older adults. This highlights that the effects of toxins on cognitive function are not limited to children but can extend to people of all ages.

Although we just touched on lead and mercury, protecting against exposure to all toxins is crucial for maintaining healthy cognitive abilities.

Environmental influences are potent determinants of cognitive function. Pollution, living conditions, and exposure to toxins can all significantly impact our mental abilities, with adverse consequences for individuals and society as a whole. Understanding these environmental factors and their effects on cognitive health is crucial for developing strategies to promote healthy brain development and mitigate the risks associated with environmental challenges.

SLEEP AND COGNITIVE FUNCTION

Sleep is a fundamental aspect of our daily lives, playing a crucial role in maintaining optimal cognitive function and overall well-being. While we often take it for granted, the quality and quantity of our sleep have a profound impact on our brain health and cognitive abilities. In this section, we will explore the connection between sleep and cognitive function, examining sleep patterns and their effects on brain health, as well as strategies to improve sleep quality.

When it comes to sleep, our brains are more active than one might think. During different stages of the sleep cycle, our brain undergoes various processes that are essential for memory consolidation, learning, problem-solving, and emotional regulation. One key aspect of sleep is the Rapid Eye Movement (REM) stage, during which our brains are highly active, resembling wakefulness in many ways. Studies have shown that REM sleep is critical for memory processing and emotional regulation, allowing us to process and understand complex information while also helping us adapt to stressful situations.

Our sleep patterns play a significant role in maintaining cognitive function. The circadian rhythm, often referred to as our internal body clock, regulates our sleep-wake cycle and influences alertness and cognitive performance throughout the day. Disruptions to this rhythm, such as shift work or irregular sleep patterns, can lead to sleep deprivation, which has been linked to decreased attention, slower reaction times, and impaired decision-making. A study published in the journal "Sleep" in 2017 highlighted the impact of sleep fragmentation on cognitive function, revealing that fragmented sleep patterns can lead to deficits in attention and memory.

Moreover, the amount of sleep we get also matters. Chronic sleep deprivation, defined as consistently getting less than the recommended 7-9 hours of sleep for adults, can have detrimental effects on cognitive abilities. A study conducted by the University of California, Irvine, in 2020 found that insufficient sleep not only impairs memory consolidation but also affects the brain's ability to clear out toxic waste products, potentially increasing the risk of neurodegenerative diseases like Alzheimer's.

Now, let's explore strategies to improve sleep quality and, consequently, cognitive function. Establishing a consistent sleep schedule is key to aligning our internal body clock and improving sleep patterns. This means going to bed and waking up at the same time each day, even on weekends. Additionally, creating a comfortable sleep environment with a dark, quiet, cool room and a comfortable mattress can help promote better sleep quality.

Limiting screen time before bed is another important strategy. The blue light emitted by phones, tablets, and computers can interfere with the production of melatonin, a hormone that regulates sleep. It's recommended to avoid screens at least an hour before bedtime to facilitate a smoother transition into sleep.

Lastly, practicing relaxation techniques like meditation, deep breathing exercises, or progressive muscle relaxation can help reduce stress and anxiety, which are common sleep disruptors. These techniques can calm the mind and prepare the body for a restful night's sleep.

Sleep is intricately linked to cognitive function, with sleep patterns and the amount of sleep we get significantly impacting our brain health and cognitive abilities. By understanding these connections and implementing strategies to improve sleep quality, we can enhance our cognitive performance and overall well-being.

NUTRITION AND COGNITIVE HEALTH

Nutrition plays a crucial role in our overall health, and its impact extends to our cognitive well-being. The connection between what we eat and our brain health is a fascinating area of research that has gained significant attention in recent years.

Let's start with some key nutrients. These are like building blocks for your brain's health and function. They provide the support your brain needs to stay sharp and focused.

Omega-3 fatty acids are the healthy fats, commonly found in fatty fish like salmon and walnuts. They are like superheroes for your brain. Studies have shown that omega-3s can improve memory and help protect against cognitive decline. They do this by maintaining the structure of your brain cells and supporting communication between them.

Next up are the B vitamins, particularly B12 and folate, which play a crucial role in brain health. A deficiency in vitamin B12, for example, can lead to memory problems and cognitive decline. Studies have linked low levels of B vitamins with a higher risk of developing age-related cognitive issues.

Vitamin D is another nutrient that deserves attention. It's not just about strong bones. Research has shown that low vitamin D levels are associated with a higher risk of cognitive decline. So spend some time in the sun and including vitamin D-rich foods like fortified dairy products and fatty fish in your diet.

Antioxidants like vitamins C and E are also important for cognitive health. These nutrients help protect your brain from oxidative stress, which can damage brain cells over time. Foods like citrus fruits, berries, and nuts are excellent sources of antioxidants.

Finally, don't forget about iron. Iron is essential for transporting oxygen to your brain and without enough of it, your brain may not get the oxygen it needs to work properly. Iron-rich foods like lean meats, beans, and spinach can help ensure your brain gets the oxygen it requires.

Now, the way to get these key nutrients is with a brain-healthy diet. One of the most well-known approaches is the Mediterranean diet, which is thought to provide essential nutrients and antioxidants that protect the brain from oxidative stress and inflammation. This dietary pattern is rich in fruits, vegetables, whole grains, lean proteins, and healthy fats like olive oil. Research published in the journal "Neurology" in 2015 found that adherence to the Mediterranean diet was associated with a lower risk of cognitive decline and a reduced risk of developing Alzheimer's disease.

But if you don't want to follow the Mediterranean Diet, you can still reap the benefits of brain boosting foods simply by eating them regularly. Here are some to take note of.

First up, we have fatty fish like salmon, trout, and sardines. These fish are rich in omega-3 fatty acids, which are like superfood for your brain. Studies have shown that omega-3s can help improve memory and protect against cognitive decline. They also support the structure of your brain cells and help with communication between them.

Next on the list are berries, especially blueberries. They are packed with antioxidants called flavonoids, which can help improve brain function. Research suggests that regular consumption of berries may delay brain aging and enhance memory. Plus, they're delicious!

Green leafy vegetables like spinach, kale, and broccoli are also fantastic for your brain. They are loaded with vitamins, minerals, and antioxidants. These nutrients help reduce the risk of cognitive decline and keep your brain sharp as you age. One study even found that eating one to two servings of leafy greens a day can help slow down cognitive decline.

Nuts and seeds are another brain-boosting option. They are rich in vitamin E, which has been linked to better cognitive performance in older adults. Additionally, nuts and seeds provide healthy fats, fiber, and other essential nutrients that support overall brain health.

Whole grains, like oats, brown rice, and quinoa, are excellent for maintaining steady energy levels in your brain. They release glucose slowly into your bloodstream, providing a steady supply of fuel for your brain. This helps improve focus and concentration.

Avocados are a unique addition to the brain-healthy list. They contain monounsaturated fats that help improve blood flow, which is vital for a healthy brain. They also have potassium and folate, which support brain function and development.

Last but not least, dark chocolate, in moderation, can be a treat for your brain. It contains flavonoids, similar to those in berries, that can boost memory and improve mood. Look for dark chocolate with a high cocoa content for the most benefits.

Whole Foods are the best way to get the nutrients you need, but sometimes we need a little help. That's where supplements come in. While some supplements have gained popularity for their potential benefits, it's important to approach them with caution and understanding.

One commonly used non-prescription supplement is Ginkgo biloba. Ginkgo is derived from the leaves of the Ginkgo biloba tree and has been marketed as a memory enhancer. However, the scientific evidence supporting its effectiveness is mixed. Some studies suggest that Ginkgo may have a modest impact on cognitive function and memory, particularly in older adults. Still, the results are not consistent across all research, and more rigorous studies are needed to establish its true benefits.

Another supplement that has gained attention is omega-3 fatty acids, usually found in fish oil capsules. As mentioned earlier, omega-3s are essential for brain health. Some studies have suggested that omega-3 supplements may help reduce the risk of cognitive decline, especially in those with lower dietary intake of these fatty acids. However, the effectiveness of supplements versus obtaining omega-3s from whole foods like fish is a subject of ongoing research.

Turmeric and its active compound, curcumin, have also been studied for their potential cognitive benefits. Turmeric has anti-inflammatory and antioxidant properties, which could be beneficial for brain health. Some research suggests that curcumin may help improve memory and cognitive function, but more studies are needed to confirm these findings and determine the optimal dosage.

Phosphatidylserine (PS) is a naturally occurring phospholipid found in high concentrations in the brain. Some studies have explored the use of PS supplements for cognitive support, particularly in older adults. Research suggests that PS may have a modest positive impact on memory and cognitive function, but again, results vary between studies.

Acetyl-L-carnitine (ALC) is another non-prescription supplement that has been investigated for its potential cognitive benefits. ALC is involved in energy production within brain cells. Some research has suggested that ALC supplements may improve cognitive function, particularly in individuals with age-related cognitive decline. However, like many supplements, the results are not consistent across all studies.

Non-prescription supplements are widely available and often marketed as tools to enhance cognitive health. If you are considering using any non-prescription supplements for cognitive health, it's essential to consult with a healthcare professional to ensure they are safe and appropriate for your individual needs.

Nutrition is a fundamental aspect of cognitive health. Brain-healthy diets like the Mediterranean diet, rich in nutrients and antioxidants, can support cognitive function and reduce the risk of cognitive decline. Key nutrients, such as omega-3 fatty acids and vitamins, play essential roles in maintaining brain health. While non-prescription supplements may hold promise, their efficacy and safety should be carefully considered in consultation with a healthcare provider.

PHYSICAL ACTIVITY AND COGNITIVE HEALTH

Physical activity is not only beneficial for maintaining physical health but also plays a significant role in preserving cognitive function as we age. In this section, we will explore how physical activity influences cognition and will also provide some basic exercise recommendations for the betterment of cognitive health.

Numerous studies have demonstrated the positive impact of physical activity on cognitive decline. Exercise increases blood flow to the brain, which can improve memory and cognitive function. A study published in the journal "Neurology" in 2012 found that regular physical activity, such as walking, was associated with a reduced risk of cognitive impairment in older adults. Furthermore, exercise has been shown to stimulate the release of neurotransmitters like dopamine and serotonin, which can enhance mood and cognitive performance. These findings suggest that staying active can help maintain cognitive function and potentially reduce the risk of conditions like dementia.

Moreover, exercise appears to have specific effects on different cognitive domains.

Aerobic exercise, like jogging or swimming, has been shown to have a positive impact on our attention and processing speed. One of the key ways it does this is by increasing blood flow to the brain. When we engage in aerobic activities, our heart pumps more blood, which carries oxygen and nutrients to the brain. This improved blood flow can help the brain work better.

In a study published in the journal "Psychology of Sport and Exercise" in 2018, researchers found that just 30 minutes of aerobic exercise, like brisk walking or cycling, can enhance attention and concentration. This means that after doing aerobic exercise, you might find it easier to focus on tasks and stay alert. It's like giving your brain a little boost to help it perform at its best.

Another way aerobic exercise helps with attention and processing speed is by increasing the production of certain chemicals in the brain, like neurotransmitters. These chemicals play a crucial role in how our brain cells communicate with each other. For example, exercise can stimulate the release of dopamine and norepinephrine, which are associated with improved attention and mood. This is why you might feel more alert and positive after a good workout.

Moreover, aerobic exercise has been linked to the growth of new brain cells in a region called the hippocampus, which is involved in memory and learning. This growth, known as neurogenesis, can help improve cognitive functions, including processing speed.

Resistance training, which involves activities like weightlifting and bodyweight exercises, has shown a connection to improved problem-solving and decision-making abilities by stimulating the release of certain brain chemicals, like brain-derived neurotrophic factor (BDNF). BDNF is a protein that supports the growth and maintenance of brain cells. When you engage in resistance training, your body produces more BDNF, which can help improve cognitive functions.

Additionally, resistance training can contribute to better overall physical health. When you are physically fit and strong, your body is better equipped to handle stress and challenges. This improved physical condition can translate into better mental resilience, which is essential for effective problem-solving and decision-making. A study published in the "Journal of Strength and Conditioning Research" in 2018 showed that resistance training improved not only muscle strength but also decision-making in older adults.

Furthermore, resistance training can have a positive impact on mood and reduce stress. When you feel less stressed and in a better mood, your cognitive abilities, including problem-solving and decision-making, tend to perform at their best.

To reap the cognitive benefits of physical activity, it's essential to incorporate regular exercise into your routine. The American Heart Association recommends at least 150 minutes of moderate-intensity aerobic activity or 75 minutes of vigorous-intensity aerobic activity per week for adults. This can include activities like brisk walking, cycling, or dancing. Additionally, muscle-strengthening activities, such as lifting weights or doing bodyweight exercises, should be performed on at least two days a week.

It's important to start slowly and gradually increase the intensity and duration of your workouts, especially if you are new to exercise or have any underlying health conditions. Consistency is key; aim for a routine that you can maintain over the long term.

MENTAL STIMULATION AND COGNITIVE RESERVE

Mental stimulation and cognitive reserve are essential concepts in understanding how our brains stay sharp and resilient throughout our lives. These ideas highlight the importance of keeping our minds active and engaged to maintain cognitive health as we age. Let's dive deeper into this fascinating topic, starting with brain-training exercises and the role they play in enhancing mental stimulation and cognitive reserve.

Brain-training exercises are activities designed to challenge and stimulate various cognitive functions, such as memory, attention, and problem-solving skills. Research has shown that engaging in regular brain-training exercises can lead to improvements in these cognitive abilities. For instance, a study published in the journal "Psychological Science" in 2013 found that older adults who participated in brain-training exercises showed better memory and reasoning skills compared to those who did not engage in such activities. These exercises can include puzzles, memory games, and even certain video games specifically designed to target cognitive functions. Let's explore some examples of brain training exercises, understanding why they work and how to incorporate them into your routine.

Sudoku and crossword puzzles are popular brain games that have been shown to have positive effects on cognition. These puzzles engage various cognitive functions, including memory, attention, and problem-solving skills, which can lead to cognitive improvement.

Firstly, Sudoku and crossword puzzles are effective because they require you to remember and process information. When you play Sudoku, you must remember which numbers you've already used in a row, column, or grid. In crossword puzzles, you need to recall the clues and answers to fill in the grid correctly. This constant mental exercise of memory helps improve your ability to remember things in your daily life.

Secondly, these puzzles promote sustained attention. To complete a Sudoku or crossword puzzle, you must stay focused on the task for an extended period. This sustained attention helps improve your ability to concentrate on other activities as well. Research has shown that enhancing attention through puzzles can have a positive impact on overall cognitive function. The consistent practice of focusing on these puzzles can train your brain to maintain attention and stay engaged in various tasks.

Additionally, Sudoku and crossword puzzles are excellent for honing your problem-solving skills. They require you to analyze patterns, deduce the correct answers, and think critically. These problem-solving exercises can carry over into real-life situations, where similar skills are often needed.

To incorporate Sudoku and crossword puzzles into your routine, start with puzzles that match your skill level. Gradually progress to more challenging ones as your abilities improve. Consistency is key, so make it a habit to solve puzzles regularly, whether it's in a dedicated puzzle book or through online platforms.

Brain training apps have gained popularity for their potential to improve cognition. These apps are designed to provide mental exercises that challenge various aspects of cognitive function, such as memory, attention, and problem-solving. They offer a convenient and accessible way to engage in cognitive exercises.

You can access these apps on your smartphone or tablet, making it easy to incorporate them into your daily routine. This accessibility encourages regular practice, which is essential for cognitive improvement.

These apps are effective because they provide targeted exercises for specific cognitive skills. For example, some apps focus on memory enhancement by presenting users with memory challenges, while others concentrate on improving attention through various tasks. By tailoring exercises to specific cognitive functions, brain training apps allow you to work on areas where you may want to see improvement.

Additionally, many brain training apps employ the principles of gamification, making the exercises engaging and enjoyable. Gamification involves incorporating game-like elements, such as rewards, challenges, and progress tracking, into the app's design. This gamified approach can motivate users to continue using the app regularly and stay committed to their cognitive training.

Moreover, brain training apps often adapt to your performance level. As you progress in your training, these apps adjust the difficulty of the exercises to keep them challenging but achievable. This adaptive feature ensures that you continue to stimulate your cognitive abilities as you improve, preventing plateaus in your cognitive growth.

Please note that the effectiveness of specific brain training apps may vary, and it's essential to choose reputable apps that are based on scientific principles and evidence-based practices for the best results. A few to look into are Lumosity, Elevate, and Peak.

Meditation and mindfulness practices have also been recognized for their positive effects on cognition and overall mental well-being. These techniques involve focusing your attention, calming your mind, and being fully present in the moment.

In meditation, you learn to focus your mind on a specific point, such as your breath or a mantra. Through consistent practice, you train your brain to remain attentive and resist distractions. This improved attention span can have a significant impact on your cognitive abilities, as it allows you to better absorb and process information in various situations.

Meditation and mindfulness can also reduce stress and anxiety. High levels of stress can impair memory, decision-making, and problem-solving abilities. By incorporating meditation and mindfulness into your daily routine, you can manage stress more effectively and create a calmer mental environment that promotes optimal cognitive performance.

Additionally, research published in the journal "Psychological Science" in 2013 showed that individuals who engaged in mindfulness meditation exhibited improvements in working memory capacity, which is essential for tasks that require holding and manipulating information in your mind.

Finally, meditation and mindfulness have been linked to increased creativity. When you clear your mind of distractions and worries, you create a fertile ground for creative thinking and improve creative problem-solving skills. By fostering a creative mindset, you can approach challenges with innovative solutions.

Learning to play a musical instrument is a rewarding endeavor that can have several positive effects on cognition. When you read sheet music or memorize melodies, your brain engages in the process of encoding and retaining information. Regular practice reinforces your memory skills as you remember musical notes, chords, and rhythm patterns.

Mastering a musical instrument also improves your fine motor skills and hand-eye coordination. Whether you're strumming a guitar, playing piano keys, or manipulating the strings of a violin, you're refining your ability to control your hands and fingers precisely.

Additionally, learning an instrument involves problem-solving. As you navigate the complexities of music, you encounter challenges like deciphering complex musical compositions or adapting to unexpected changes while performing. These problem-solving experiences stimulate your brain's analytical and critical thinking processes, fostering better decision-making abilities.

Finally, playing a musical instrument encourages creativity and emotional expression. When you play music, you tap into your artistic side, using your instrument as a medium to convey emotions and tell stories. This creative outlet can boost your mood, reduce stress, and enhance your overall emotional well-being. As a result, you may find yourself better equipped to handle emotional challenges and stressors in daily life.

The last example of a brain training exercise is language learning. Learning a new language is not only about acquiring a new means of communication; it also engages your brain in complex mental exercises. When you study a new language, you must memorize vocabulary, understand grammar rules, and practice pronunciation. These tasks require memory, attention, and problem-solving skills, all of which give your brain a robust cognitive workout.

The process of switching between languages also enhances your brain's flexibility and adaptability. This cognitive flexibility, known as code-switching, trains your brain to manage multiple tasks and priorities simultaneously. As a result, you may find it easier to juggle various responsibilities in your daily life, from work to personal activities.

Additionally, learning a new language enhances your listening and communication skills. When you practice listening and speaking in a foreign language, you must pay close attention to nuances in pronunciation and intonation. This heightened awareness of auditory cues can improve your overall listening skills and your ability to understand others in noisy or challenging environments.

And lastly, language learning fosters cultural awareness and empathy. Exploring a new language often involves delving into the culture and customs of the people who speak it. This cultural immersion can broaden your perspective, enhance your empathy for others, and improve your ability to understand different points of view. These skills are not only valuable in interpersonal relationships but also in various professional settings.

Incorporating these brain training exercises into your daily routine can be a fun and rewarding way to keep your mind active and agile. However, it's important to note that the effectiveness of brain-training exercises can vary from person to person, and not all studies have yielded consistent results. Some critics argue that the benefits of these exercises may not transfer to real-life situations, but many individuals still find them enjoyable and mentally stimulating.

Remember to start gradually, stay consistent, and challenge yourself progressively to reap the cognitive benefits these activities offer.

Now let's talk about the concept of lifelong learning, which is the practice of continually acquiring new knowledge and skills throughout one's life, regardless of age or formal education. Engaging in lifelong learning has been linked to cognitive resilience, which is the brain's ability to adapt, withstand challenges, and maintain optimal cognitive function as we age.

One of the primary reasons lifelong learning contributes to cognitive resilience is neuroplasticity, the brain's remarkable ability to reorganize and form new neural connections in response to learning experiences. When you engage in new learning activities, your brain is constantly challenged, promoting the creation of new neural pathways and strengthening existing ones. This adaptability helps your brain remain flexible and resilient over time.

Another key reason lifelong learning supports cognitive resilience is the mental exercise it provides. Just like physical exercise keeps your body fit, cognitive exercise through learning keeps your brain sharp. The act of grappling with new ideas, problem-solving, and critical thinking maintains cognitive function and can even improve memory and attention.

Lifelong learning also fosters social engagement, another crucial element in maintaining cognitive resilience. Interacting with others through classes, workshops, or social clubs can provide social and emotional support, reduce stress, and improve mental well-being. Studies, such as one published in "JAMA Psychiatry" in 2020, have shown that social interaction is associated with a lower risk of cognitive decline and dementia.

To embrace lifelong learning, consider exploring various avenues, such as formal education, online courses, workshops, or even self-directed learning through books and online resources. Start by identifying subjects or skills that genuinely interest you, as passion can fuel your motivation to learn. Whether it's a new language, a musical instrument, or a hobby like painting or gardening, make a commitment to consistently engage with the subject matter.

Mental stimulation and cognitive reserve are intertwined concepts that emphasize the importance of keeping our minds engaged and active throughout our lives. Brain-training exercises can be a fun and beneficial way to challenge our cognitive abilities, while lifelong learning contributes to cognitive resilience, potentially reducing the risk of cognitive decline as we age. These strategies underscore the significance of maintaining mental fitness and cognitive health as we journey through life.

STRESS AND COGNITION

The effects of stress on cognitive function are well-documented in scientific research. When we experience stress, our bodies release stress hormones like cortisol and adrenaline. While these hormones are essential for our fight-or-flight response in dangerous situations, chronic stress can lead to an overproduction of these chemicals. This excess can impair our cognitive function in various ways. Studies have shown that prolonged stress can lead to difficulties with concentration, memory problems, and decreased ability to make sound decisions. It can also affect our problem-solving skills and creativity negatively.

Furthermore, research has demonstrated that chronic stress can actually shrink the hippocampus, a region of the brain responsible for memory and learning. This structural change can result in difficulties in forming new memories and recalling information when needed. In addition, stress can lead to a state of mental fatigue, making it harder to focus on tasks, leading to decreased productivity.

Now you know how stress diminishes cognition, let's discuss some techniques for stress reduction. We have already discussed the power of exercise, nutrition, sleep, and meditation for enhancing and maintaining cognition. Getting these things right also help with stress management, but we won't go into them again.

Something we haven't talked about in depth yet are relaxation techniques other than meditation, which can be incredibly effective in reducing stress and, in turn, improving cognition.

One powerful relaxation technique is deep breathing. It's a simple practice that involves taking slow, deep breaths to calm your mind and body. Studies have shown that deep breathing can help reduce stress hormones like cortisol and increase the flow of oxygen to the brain. This increased oxygen supply can enhance cognitive function by improving focus and clarity. You can try deep breathing by inhaling slowly through your nose, counting to four, holding your breath for a moment, and then exhaling slowly through your mouth.

Progressive muscle relaxation is a technique that can help ease both physical and mental tension. It involves systematically tensing and then relaxing different muscle groups in your body. This process helps release physical stress, which, in turn, can lead to reduced mental stress.

Yoga is another relaxation method that combines physical postures, breathing exercises, and meditation. It has been shown to reduce stress and anxiety while enhancing cognitive function. Some research indicates that regular yoga practice can boost memory, attention, and processing speed. The mind-body connection in yoga helps create a sense of calm that can carry over into daily life, reducing the impact of stress on your cognitive abilities.

Stress management plays a crucial role in preserving our cognitive function. The impact of stress on our ability to think, remember, and make decisions should not be underestimated. However, with the adoption of effective stress reduction techniques such as relaxation practices, exercise, and a healthy lifestyle, we can minimize these negative effects and maintain our cognitive abilities even in the face of life's challenges.

SOCIAL ENGAGEMENT AND COGNITIVE HEALTH

Social engagement involves our interactions with friends, family, and the broader community, encompassing everything from casual conversations to deep emotional connections. The impact of social engagement on cognitive health has been extensively studied, and the results consistently highlight its positive effects.

One of the key benefits is that it helps to keep our minds active and engaged. When we engage in conversations, discussions, and social activities, our brains are constantly processing information, solving problems, and making decisions. This mental stimulation is akin to exercise for the brain, helping to maintain its cognitive functions and even potentially slowing down age-related decline.

Social engagement is not only about chatting and mingling; it also has a significant impact on our emotional well-being, which, in turn, plays a crucial role in maintaining cognitive health. Research has shown that positive emotions and emotional stability have a direct connection to our cognitive abilities. When we engage in social interactions that make us feel happy, connected, and emotionally secure, we are nurturing our emotional well-being, and this can have positive effects on our brain.

Numerous studies have established a strong link between emotional well-being and cognitive health. For instance, a study published in the journal "Psychological Science" in 2013 found that people who reported higher levels of emotional well-being, such as feelings of happiness, contentment, and satisfaction with life, also tended to perform better on cognitive tasks. This suggests that when we are in a good emotional state, our brain functions more effectively.

When we interact with friends, family, or even acquaintances, we often experience positive emotions like joy, laughter, and a sense of belonging. These interactions reduce feelings of loneliness and isolation, which are known to have detrimental effects on emotional well-being and cognitive health. When we feel connected to others and experience positive emotions, it releases neurochemicals in our brains, such as dopamine and oxytocin, that contribute to feelings of happiness and emotional stability.

Moreover, social engagement provides a support system that can help us cope with stress and adversity. Having someone to talk to and lean on during difficult times can reduce the negative impact of stress on our emotional well-being. When we are less stressed and anxious, our cognitive functions, such as memory and problem-solving, tend to work better.

Here are some practical tips to help you build and maintain positive social connections.

Firstly, staying active in your community can be a great way to foster social connections. Engaging in local clubs, groups, or events that align with your interests allows you to meet new people who share your passions. For example, joining a book club, a gardening group, or a sports team can provide opportunities to connect with others who have similar hobbies or interests.

Secondly, it's important to prioritize quality relationships over quantity. While having a wide network of acquaintances can be valuable, focusing on a few meaningful relationships can be particularly beneficial. Strong emotional connections tend to have a more substantial impact on cognitive health.

Using technology wisely can also help maintain social connections. Social interactions are not limited to face-to-face encounters. You can stay in touch with friends and family through social media, video calls, or messaging apps. However, it's essential to be mindful of excessive screen time, as studies have shown that excessive use of technology can have adverse effects on mental health and may negatively impact real-life interactions.

Volunteering is another effective way to build and maintain social connections. By volunteering for a cause you care about, you not only give back to the community but also connect with like-minded individuals who share your values.

Lastly, being a good listener is a crucial aspect of maintaining meaningful social connections. Engaging in meaningful conversations involves active listening. Show genuine interest in what others have to say, ask questions, and practice empathy.

MEMORY IMPROVEMENT TECHNIQUES

In a world filled with vast amounts of information, improving memory can have significant benefits in various aspects of life, from academic performance to professional success and even in day-to-day activities. Two commonly employed memory improvement techniques are mnemonic devices and memory training exercises, each offering distinct approaches to bolstering memory function.

Mnemonic devices are memory aids that use various strategies to make information more memorable. They work by organizing information in a way that's easier for your brain to grasp and recall later. One popular mnemonic device is the method of loci. In this technique, you imagine a familiar place, like your home, and associate the items you want to remember with specific locations within that place. For example, if you need to remember a shopping list, you might picture a loaf of bread on your doorstep, a carton of milk on your couch, and so on. A study conducted by Röer, Bell, and Buchner in 2013 found that using the method of loci improved participants' ability to remember lists of words.

Acronyms and acrostics are another set of mnemonic devices. Acronyms are words or phrases created by taking the initial letters of the things you want to remember. For instance, "ROYGBIV" helps us recall the colors of the rainbow: red, orange, yellow, green, blue, indigo, and violet. Acrostics, on the other hand, involve creating a sentence or phrase where each word's first letter corresponds to the items you need to remember. These devices provide a structured and memorable way to encode information in your brain, making it easier to retrieve later.

Chunking is yet another mnemonic strategy. It involves breaking down long lists or strings of information into smaller, more manageable chunks. For instance, instead of trying to remember a 16-digit credit card number as one long sequence, you can group it into four sets of four digits each.

Rhymes and songs are also effective mnemonic devices, particularly for remembering sequences or orders. Many of us still use the "ABC" song we learned as children to remember the order of letters in the alphabet. The rhythm and melody make the information stick in our minds.

Memory training methods are techniques designed to enhance your memory skills through practice and specific exercises. These methods are based on the idea that, like any other skill, memory can be improved with consistent training. One popular memory training method is the Dual N-Back task, which targets working memory—the part of your memory responsible for holding and manipulating information in your mind temporarily.

The Dual N-Back task involves remembering two things simultaneously: visual and auditory stimuli. For example, you might hear a series of letters and see a grid with squares lighting up in different positions. Your job is to remember both the letters and the positions of the squares, and whenever a letter or square matches the one presented a certain number of steps back, you press a button. This task challenges your working memory and cognitive abilities.

Research conducted by Susanne M. Jaeggi and her colleagues, published in the Proceedings of the National Academy of Sciences in 2008, demonstrated the effectiveness of the Dual N-Back task. Participants who regularly practiced this task showed significant improvements in their working memory and fluid intelligence over time. Fluid intelligence refers to your ability to solve problems and adapt to new situations, which is closely related to memory function.

Memory training programs like Lumosity and CogniFit offer a variety of exercises and games that target different aspects of memory, such as short-term memory, long-term memory, and spatial memory. While the effectiveness of these programs may vary from person to person, they provide structured and engaging ways to challenge and improve memory skills.

Memory improvement techniques like mnemonic devices and memory training exercises offer valuable ways to boost memory function. Mnemonic devices provide clever tricks to make information more memorable, while memory training exercises challenge and strengthen the brain's memory capabilities. Incorporating these techniques into your daily routine can lead to improved memory recall and enhance your overall cognitive abilities, ultimately benefiting various aspects of your life.

SPEED READING AND INFORMATION RETENTION

Speed reading and information retention are two crucial skills that can significantly impact one's ability to process and understand large volumes of written material efficiently. Speed reading refers to the practice of reading text at a faster rate than the average reading speed, while information retention involves the ability to remember and understand the material read.

When it comes to speed reading, one common technique is known as "chunking." This has the same name but is different to the chunking technique in the previous section.

"Chunking" in the context of speed reading involves grouping words or phrases together instead of reading each word individually. Studies have shown that skilled readers tend to use this technique naturally, allowing them to process more information in less time. Additionally, using a pointer or guide, such as your finger or a pen, can help improve reading speed by keeping your eyes on track and reducing the chances of regression, where you go back and reread previous parts of the text. A study conducted by the University of Reading in 2016 found that using a pointer increased reading speed without compromising comprehension.

Another technique used in speed reading is eliminating subvocalization, which is the habit of silently pronouncing each word as you read, which can significantly slow down reading speed.

While speed reading can help process information faster, it's equally important to retain and comprehend the material. One effective strategy for enhancing comprehension is active engagement with the text. This means asking questions as you read, making predictions about what will come next, and summarizing key points. A study conducted by the University of Washington in 2020 found that actively engaging with the text led to better comprehension and retention compared to passive reading.

Furthermore, visualization can be a powerful tool for improving comprehension. When readers create mental images of the content they are reading, it helps them better understand and remember the information.

CRITICAL THINKING AND LOGICAL REASONING

Critical thinking and logical reasoning are essential cognitive skills that enable individuals to analyze, evaluate, and solve problems systematically. They form the foundation of sound decision-making, allowing us to navigate the complexities of the world around us.

The development of these skills is a continuous process that involves various techniques and approaches. Engaging in debates or discussions is a powerful method. When you participate in debates or discussions, you're given a chance to research and understand different sides of an issue, which is a crucial aspect of critical thinking. When you have to defend your position or counter someone else's argument, you're forced to think carefully about the evidence and reasons behind your beliefs.

Furthermore, when you have to present your ideas clearly and persuasively, it not only sharpens your critical thinking but also your communication skills. This is essential in both academic and real-world settings. You'll be better equipped to express your thoughts and opinions effectively.

Debates and discussions also foster an environment where you can learn from others. Listening to different perspectives and challenging your own beliefs can broaden your understanding of complex issues. It encourages open-mindedness and helps you develop empathy, a valuable skill in critical thinking. By considering various viewpoints, you become better at evaluating arguments and making informed decisions.

Reading and analyzing complex texts, such as literature or scientific papers, is another excellent way to enhance critical thinking skills. When you read complex texts, you're exposed to diverse ideas and viewpoints. This challenges your mind to think critically about the information presented. You learn to evaluate the evidence, assess arguments, and consider the credibility of the sources, which are all essential aspects of critical thinking.

Moreover, literature and scientific papers often present complex ideas and arguments. Analyzing them requires you to break down the content, identify key concepts, and connect them to form a coherent understanding. This process encourages you to think deeply and critically about the material. For instance, when reading a scientific paper, you might need to question the methodology, validity of results, and implications of the study. This analytical approach sharpens your critical thinking skills.

Complex texts also often contain ambiguity and uncertainty, which are inherent to many real-world problems. When you encounter such elements, it challenges you to think critically, consider various interpretations, and make informed judgments. This ability to navigate uncertainty is invaluable in decision-making and problem-solving, making you a more effective critical thinker.

Problem-based learning is yet another approach to enhance critical thinking skills by encouraging learners to inquire, analyze data, and evaluate possible solutions. In problem-based learning, you're given a challenging problem or scenario to work on, often in a group. You must research and gather information, brainstorm ideas, and come up with potential solutions. This process mirrors how critical thinking works in the real world, where you need to analyze information, assess options, and make informed decisions.

One of the key aspects of problem-based learning is that it promotes active learning. Instead of just passively receiving information, you're actively engaged in finding solutions to complex problems. This active involvement sharpens your critical thinking skills by making you think deeply about the problem, consider different perspectives, and weigh the pros and cons of various solutions.

Furthermore, problem-based learning encourages collaboration. You work with others in a team to tackle the problem, which means you get to hear different viewpoints and ideas. This collaboration helps you develop the ability to critically evaluate and integrate diverse perspectives into your problem-solving process.

Another benefit of problem-based learning is that it often involves open-ended problems with no single "right" answer. This challenges you to think critically and creatively to find solutions. You learn to tolerate ambiguity and uncertainty, skills that are crucial in real-life situations where problems aren't always neatly defined.

The last method for enhancing critical thinking skills we will discuss is the Socratic method. This method is named after the ancient Greek philosopher Socrates, who used it to stimulate deep thinking and encourage people to question their beliefs and ideas.

One of the key features of the Socratic method is the use of open-ended questions. Instead of giving direct answers, the Socratic teacher or facilitator asks questions that challenge students' thinking. These questions require students to analyze, evaluate, and defend their ideas and arguments, which encourages active engagement and reflection. When students are faced with thought-provoking questions, they must think critically about their responses. They can't simply rely on memorized information but are pushed to consider the reasoning behind their beliefs. This process of self-examination and reflection is a fundamental aspect of critical thinking.

The Socratic method also promotes dialogue and discussion. It creates an environment where students are encouraged to share their thoughts, listen to others, and explore various perspectives on a topic. This collaborative aspect of the Socratic method helps students develop empathy. They learn to appreciate different viewpoints and evaluate arguments from multiple angles.

Finally, the Socratic method teaches students to question assumptions. It challenges preconceived notions and encourages a healthy skepticism. This is essential in critical thinking because it helps individuals avoid accepting information uncritically and instead, seek evidence and reasoning behind claims.

CREATIVITY AND PROBLEM-SOLVING

Creativity and problem-solving are essential skills in both our personal and professional lives. They go hand in hand, as creative thinking often plays a pivotal role in finding innovative solutions to complex problems.

Divergent thinking is a key concept when it comes to boosting creativity. It's a way of thinking that encourages us to generate many different ideas or solutions to a problem without being restricted by conventional or logical constraints.

Research by J.P. Guilford in 1950 is often cited as a foundational study on divergent thinking. Guilford's work suggested that there are different aspects of thinking, divergent thinking being one of them. It involves coming up with multiple answers to a single question or problem. For example, if you were asked to think of uses for a paperclip beyond just holding papers together, divergent thinking would encourage you to brainstorm a wide variety of creative ideas, like using it as a hook for small items or a makeshift bookmark.

Divergent thinking encourages us to explore a wide range of possibilities, even if some of those ideas might seem strange or unconventional at first. This is important because creativity often emerges from unexpected connections and novel combinations of ideas. A study published in the journal "Creativity Research Journal" (Dahl, D. W., et al., 2003) found that individuals who engaged in divergent thinking exercises generated more creative ideas than those who followed a more structured, convergent thinking approach.

Moreover, divergent thinking is not limited to artistic or creative endeavors; it can be applied in various areas of life and problem-solving. Whether you're trying to brainstorm new marketing strategies, find alternative solutions to a technical issue, or even plan an innovative menu for a restaurant, divergent thinking can be a valuable tool.

Mindfulness meditation has come up several times already, and here it makes another appearance because although it's often associated with reducing stress and enhancing well-being, research has also shown its positive impact on creativity.

A study published in the journal "Psychological Science" involved participants engaging in a short meditation session and then completing creative thinking tasks. The results showed that those who had practiced mindfulness exhibited greater divergent thinking, which as just explained, is the ability to generate multiple creative ideas or solutions to a problem.

The link between mindfulness meditation and creativity can be explained by how this practice changes our mental state. Mindfulness helps individuals become more aware of their thoughts and feelings, reducing distractions and the mental clutter that can stifle creativity. By focusing on the present moment, people can gain clarity of thought and create a mental space that is conducive to creative thinking.

Moreover, mindfulness meditation can enhance the ability to connect seemingly unrelated ideas, which is a hallmark of creative thinking. When individuals engage in mindfulness, they become better at recognizing patterns, identifying relationships between concepts, and seeing novel connections between ideas. This mental flexibility can be a powerful catalyst for creativity.

In addition to its immediate effects, a study in the journal "Frontiers in Psychology" suggests that individuals who engage in mindfulness meditation over an extended period tend to experience lasting improvements in creativity and problem-solving abilities.

Embracing constraints is an interesting approach to boosting creativity. It might seem counterintuitive, but research and real-life examples have shown that limitations or constraints can actually inspire innovative thinking. This is because when people face restrictions or boundaries, they are encouraged to find creative solutions within those limitations.

One notable example comes from the world of art. The poet Theodor Geisel, better known as Dr. Seuss, wrote one of his most famous books, "Green Eggs and Ham," using only 50 different words. This constraint forced him to be incredibly creative with his language choices, resulting in a beloved and highly creative children's book. This demonstrates that embracing constraints can lead to remarkable creativity.

In the business world, constraints can also lead to inventive solutions. A study published in the journal "Psychological Science" found that when teams faced external constraints or challenges, they often became more creative in their problem-solving efforts. Constraints can act as a catalyst, pushing individuals and teams to think outside the box and find new approaches.

Constraints can be particularly useful in encouraging resourcefulness and efficiency. When resources are limited, individuals often come up with creative ways to make the most of what they have. This can be seen in various fields, from architecture and design to engineering and software development. Necessity can be a powerful driver of creativity.

Another way to boost creativity is to expose yourself to diverse experiences and ideas. This is like giving your mind a treasure trove of inspiration to draw from. Research has shown that people who engage in a wide range of activities and seek out different perspectives are more likely to come up with creative solutions to problems.

When you encounter new ideas, cultures, and ways of thinking, your mind accumulates a wealth of resources to fuel creativity. This means that the more you explore, the more creative your thinking can become.

Moreover, diversity in experiences and ideas helps break down mental barriers and encourages thinking outside the box. When you immerse yourself in different worlds, you start to see connections and patterns that others might miss. This fresh perspective can lead to innovative solutions and creative breakthroughs.

Interacting with people from diverse backgrounds is another aspect of this. Research in the "Journal of Applied Psychology" has shown that diverse teams tend to generate more creative ideas than homogeneous groups.

Furthermore, exploring diverse experiences and ideas can help you adapt to changing situations and stay flexible in your thinking. This adaptability is essential for creative problem-solving and staying ahead of the curve.

Incorporating breaks into your work or creative process can also be beneficial. When our minds are constantly focused on a task or problem, we can become mentally fatigued, and our thinking can become rigid. Taking a quick break, whether it's going for a walk, doing a simple repetitive task, or just sitting quietly for a few minutes, give your brain the breathing space it needs to generate fresh ideas and innovative solutions.

Mind-wandering, often seen as daydreaming, involves letting your thoughts flow freely without a specific goal or focus. During these moments, your mind can make unexpected connections and associations between seemingly unrelated ideas. This can lead to creative insights and solutions that may not have emerged when you were actively concentrating on a problem.

Furthermore, taking breaks can also help with problem-solving by allowing your brain to subconsciously process information. Research has shown that our brains continue working on unresolved problems in the background when we take breaks. This phenomenon is often referred to as the "incubation period."

Speaking of problem solving, the problem-solving cycle is a structured approach that plays a significant role in effective problem-solving. It's like a roadmap that helps individuals and teams navigate complex problems step by step. This method was popularized by George Polya in his book "How to Solve It" in 1945, and research has shown that it can lead to more successful outcomes in tackling a wide range of problems.

The first step in the problem-solving cycle is understanding the problem. This involves taking the time to clearly define the problem, gather all relevant information, and analyze the situation. This sets the stage for the rest of the process.

Once the problem is understood, the next step is to devise a plan. This is where you brainstorm different approaches and strategies to address the problem.

After devising a plan, it's time to put it into action, which is the third step in the problem-solving cycle. This involves implementing the chosen solution or strategy. Sometimes, this phase may reveal unexpected challenges or require adjustments to the plan.

The final step in the cycle is evaluating the results. After implementing the plan, it's essential to assess whether the solution has effectively addressed the problem. This evaluation phase allows for reflection and learning from the experience. By reviewing what worked and what didn't, individuals and teams can improve their problem-solving skills over time.

Collaborative problem-solving emphasizes teamwork and the collective brainstorming of ideas to find innovative solutions.

A study published in the "Journal of the Learning Sciences" highlights how working in groups can provide access to different viewpoints and a wider pool of knowledge. When people with diverse backgrounds and skills come together to tackle a problem, they can generate more creative and well-rounded solutions.

Moreover, collaborative problem-solving fosters open communication and encourages the exchange of ideas. In a collaborative setting, individuals can challenge assumptions, share their insights, and build on each other's suggestions.

Collaborative problem-solving can also enhance problem-solving skills in individuals. Studies have shown that engaging in group problem-solving activities can improve critical thinking, decision-making, and interpersonal skills. It also helps individuals develop a deeper understanding of the problem-solving process itself.

Collaborative problem-solving as a practice mirrors real-world situations where complex problems often require input from multiple stakeholders. Learning to work effectively in teams not only enhances problem-solving abilities but also prepares individuals for success in their careers and in various aspects of life.

The "5 Whys" technique is a problem-solving approach that helps get to the root cause of an issue by repeatedly asking "why" to uncover deeper layers of causation. This method is simple but powerful and has been widely used in various industries, including manufacturing and engineering. Research and case studies have shown that the "5 Whys" technique can be an effective way to identify and address the underlying causes of problems.

The idea behind the "5 Whys" technique is to dig beyond the surface-level symptoms of a problem and trace it back to its origins. Each time you ask "why," you peel back a layer and get closer to the fundamental cause. By the time you've asked "why" five times, you often arrive at a root cause that, once addressed, can prevent the problem from recurring.

Moreover, the "5 Whys" technique promotes a culture of continuous improvement. Instead of merely treating the symptoms of a problem, it encourages teams to explore deeper issues that may be contributing to the problem. This approach aligns with the principles of lean thinking, which emphasizes eliminating waste and optimizing processes.

The simplicity of the "5 Whys" technique also makes it accessible and applicable in various contexts. It can be used not only in manufacturing but also in fields such as healthcare, software development, and even personal problem-solving. The technique encourages critical thinking and helps individuals and teams gain a better understanding of the challenges they face.

The scientific method is a systematic approach to effective problem-solving and understanding the world around us. It's like a step-by-step process that scientists and researchers use to investigate and answer questions or solve problems. While it's commonly associated with scientific research, the principles of the scientific method can be applied to various aspects of problem-solving and decision-making.

The scientific method typically begins with making observations and asking questions about a specific phenomenon or problem. This step is crucial because it helps define the problem and identify what needs to be investigated.

Once the problem or question is defined, the next step is to form a hypothesis. A hypothesis is like an educated guess about what might be causing the observed phenomenon or problem. It's a statement that can be tested through experimentation or research.

The scientific method then involves conducting experiments or gathering data to test the hypothesis. This step is where empirical evidence comes into play. By systematically collecting and analyzing data, researchers can determine whether their hypothesis is supported or refuted.

Following data collection and analysis, the scientific method encourages drawing conclusions and making inferences based on the evidence. This step is essential for arriving at well-founded solutions or explanations to problems.

Finally, the scientific method includes the step of communicating the results and findings to others. This sharing of information is essential for building upon previous research, allowing others to replicate experiments or investigations, and advancing knowledge in the field.

Next, let's go over the use of decision-making tools, which provide structured frameworks for making informed choices when faced with complex decisions. There are many decision-making tools available, each with its specific application. Here we will cover a few of the more well-known ones.

The decision matrix helps individuals or teams compare and evaluate different options systematically. It's like a structured framework that allows you to weigh various factors or criteria to make informed choices. This tool has gained recognition for its ability to enhance decision-making by providing a clear method for assessing options based on specific criteria.

A study published in the "Journal of Decision Systems" highlights the effectiveness of decision matrices in multi-criteria decision analysis. By listing all the relevant criteria and assigning weights to them, individuals can objectively assess and rank the available options.

The decision matrix typically consists of a table with options listed in rows and criteria in columns. Each cell in the matrix is used to score how well each option performs on each criterion. Scores are assigned based on the importance of each criterion and the performance of each option in relation to that criterion. The tool then calculates a total score for each option, aiding in the decision-making process by identifying the most suitable choice.

One of the key advantages of the decision matrix is its ability to provide a structured and visual representation of the decision-making process. This clarity can be particularly beneficial when decisions involve complex trade-offs between various factors. It helps individuals or teams make decisions that align with their objectives and priorities.

Furthermore, the decision matrix encourages transparency and objectivity in decision-making. By explicitly defining and weighting criteria, it minimizes the influence of personal biases and ensures that decisions are based on rational assessments. This can lead to more fair and consistent decision outcomes.

Another common tool is cost-benefit analysis, which is used to assess the advantages and disadvantages of different options, especially in the fields of economics, business, and public policy. It helps individuals, organizations, and governments make informed choices by quantifying and comparing the costs and benefits associated with various alternatives.

In cost-benefit analysis, the first step is to identify and measure all the costs and benefits related to a particular decision or project. This includes not only monetary costs but also non-monetary factors like environmental impacts, social considerations, and intangible benefits. By including all relevant factors, cost-benefit analysis provides a comprehensive view of the decision's potential consequences.

A study published in the "Journal of Environmental Economics and Management" explored the application of cost-benefit analysis in environmental decision-making. The research emphasized the importance of considering environmental costs and benefits alongside economic factors, showcasing how this approach can inform sustainable decision-making.

Once all costs and benefits are identified and quantified, cost-benefit analysis involves comparing them to determine whether the benefits outweigh the costs. If the benefits are greater, the decision is considered economically viable and advantageous. This analysis can help prioritize projects, policies, or investments based on their potential for generating net benefits.

Moreover, cost-benefit analysis provides a framework for comparing different options objectively. By assigning a monetary value to various factors, it allows for apples-to-apples comparisons even when the benefits and costs are diverse. This objectivity helps ensure that decisions are based on rational assessments rather than subjective judgments.

However, it's essential to note that cost-benefit analysis has its limitations and challenges, such as assigning values to intangible factors or dealing with uncertainty. Researchers continue to explore ways to address these issues and refine the methodology to enhance its effectiveness in various decision-making contexts.

Decision trees are a versatile and visual decision-making tool that helps individuals and organizations make informed choices in situations with multiple possible outcomes and uncertainties. They are like flowcharts that map out different branches of decisions and their associated probabilities, making complex decisions more manageable. Research and practical applications have shown the value of decision trees in various fields, including business, healthcare, and finance.

In a decision tree, the decision or problem is represented as a starting point, often called the "root." From there, different options or choices are depicted as branches, leading to various possible outcomes or consequences. Each branch is associated with a probability or likelihood of occurring. This visual representation allows decision-makers to see the different paths and potential consequences of their decisions.

One of the strengths of decision trees is their ability to help decision-makers identify the most rational and cost-effective choices. By calculating the expected value of each option, which is the sum of the outcomes weighted by their probabilities, decision trees can highlight the option with the highest expected value. This can guide individuals and organizations in making decisions that maximize their objectives.

Moreover, decision trees facilitate sensitivity analysis, allowing decision-makers to assess the impact of changing probabilities or values on the decision's outcome. This feature helps in understanding the robustness of a decision under different scenarios and uncertainties, contributing to more informed and resilient decision-making.

However, it's essential to note that creating and interpreting decision trees can be complex, especially for decisions with many branches and probabilities. Nonetheless, various software tools and techniques have been developed to simplify the process and make decision trees more accessible and practical.

Finally, scenario planning. Scenario planning is a strategic decision-making tool that helps individuals, organizations, and governments anticipate and prepare for a range of possible future scenarios. It's like creating a collection of stories about different possible futures to understand potential challenges and opportunities. Research and practical applications have shown that scenario planning is a valuable approach for making decisions and developing strategies that are resilient and adaptable to a changing world.

In scenario planning, the first step is to identify key uncertainties and trends that may impact the future. These uncertainties could be related to economic, technological, social, or environmental factors. By considering a wide range of potential developments, scenario planning encourages decision-makers to think beyond their current assumptions and mental models. It fosters a proactive mindset that enables organizations to adapt and thrive in dynamic environments.

Once uncertainties and trends are identified, scenario planning involves constructing a set of scenarios. Each scenario is like a detailed narrative that describes a plausible future based on a combination of different factors and assumptions. These scenarios can range from optimistic to pessimistic, providing a spectrum of potential outcomes.

One of the strengths of scenario planning is its ability to help decision-makers test the robustness of their strategies under different scenarios. By considering how strategies perform across various future conditions, organizations can identify vulnerabilities and make adjustments to their plans. This adaptive approach contributes to better decision-making and risk management.

Moreover, scenario planning encourages collaboration and communication within organizations. It involves multiple stakeholders in the process of exploring and discussing future scenarios, fostering a shared understanding of potential challenges and opportunities. This shared perspective can lead to more coordinated and effective decision-making.

Creativity and problem-solving are foundational skills with broad applications. They empower individuals and organizations to navigate challenges, fostering innovation and adaptability. Creativity, often fueled by divergent thinking and mindfulness, leads to fresh insights and solutions. Problem-solving, guided by structured approaches and decision-making tools, enables effective decision-making. These skills are vital in personal and professional realms, enhancing resilience and the ability to thrive in diverse and ever-changing environments.

EMOTIONAL INTELLIGENCE

Emotional intelligence, often abbreviated as EQ, is a vital aspect of human psychology that plays a significant role in our personal and professional lives. It refers to the ability to recognize, understand, manage, and effectively use emotions, both in ourselves and in our interactions with others.

Understanding emotional intelligence involves recognizing and managing emotions, both in ourselves and in others. It's an essential skill for building better relationships, making sound decisions, and leading a more fulfilling life. Several key components contribute to emotional intelligence.

The first component is self-awareness. It means understanding and recognizing our own emotions. It's like having a mirror inside ourselves that shows us what we're feeling and why. Self-awareness helps us know when we're happy, sad, angry, or anxious and allows us to grasp the reasons behind those emotions.

This self-awareness is not about being overly self-critical but about being honest with ourselves. When we are self-aware, we can identify what triggers our emotions. For instance, we might realize that we get upset when we receive criticism or stressed when we have too much work to do. This understanding helps us take control of our reactions.

Studies have shown that people who are more self-aware tend to have better mental health and well-being. They can manage their emotions more effectively, which can reduce stress and anxiety. When we're aware of our emotions, we can also communicate better with others about how we're feeling, leading to healthier relationships.

Self-awareness isn't something we're born with; it's a skill that can be developed and improved over time. Journaling is a helpful and practical tool for enhancing self-awareness which involves writing down your thoughts, feelings, and experiences regularly. This practice can provide you with valuable insights into your emotions and the factors that trigger them.

When you journal, you create a space to reflect on your daily experiences. You can record how you felt in different situations, what made you happy, angry, or sad, and why you think you reacted the way you did. This process helps you become more in tune with your emotions and recognize patterns in your behavior. Over time, you'll start to see connections between your emotions and specific events or circumstances.

A study published in the journal "Psychological Science" in 2014 found that expressive writing, like journaling, can help individuals better understand and regulate their emotions. It can also lead to reduced stress and improved mood.

Journaling can also serve as a tool for problem-solving and decision-making. When you have a record of your emotions and the situations that trigger them, you can start to identify which situations are beneficial and which are not. This awareness can guide you in making choices that align with your emotional well-being and overall goals.

Moreover, journaling allows you to track your personal growth and development. You can look back at your previous entries and see how you've evolved in your emotional responses and coping strategies. This retrospective view can boost your self-confidence and motivate you to continue working on your emotional intelligence.

Once again our old friend meditation comes in to play. Through meditation, your can develop a heightened sense of self-awareness by paying attention to your thoughts, feelings, and bodily sensations. This process allows your to become more attuned to your emotional responses and understand why your feel a certain way in different situations.

One of the key benefits of meditation is the ability to gain distance from our thoughts and emotions. Instead of reacting impulsively to feelings of anger, anxiety, or sadness, meditation teaches us to observe these emotions objectively. This newfound perspective can help us make more informed choices about how to respond to challenging situations.

Moreover, meditation can improve emotional regulation, another vital aspect of emotional intelligence. Research published in the journal "Psychological Bulletin" in 2012 suggests that meditation can reduce symptoms of anxiety, depression, and stress, which are often linked to difficulties in emotional regulation.

Meditation also fosters empathy. When we become more aware of our own emotions and cultivate a compassionate attitude towards ourselves, we are better equipped to understand and connect with the emotions of others.

Engaging in open and honest conversations with trusted family members, friends, or therapists is another valuable way to enhance self-awareness. These conversations provide a supportive environment where you can explore your thoughts and emotions, gain valuable insights, and develop a deeper understanding of yourself. While there may not be specific studies focused solely on these conversations, research on therapy, communication, and social support highlights their significance.

Family members and friends can play a crucial role in helping you become more self-aware by offering a different perspective on your emotions and behaviors. These trusted individuals can provide feedback, share observations, and ask questions that encourage self-reflection. Through these interactions, you can identify patterns in your emotional responses and better comprehend the reasons behind your feelings, which contributes to improved self-awareness.

Therapists, in particular, are trained to facilitate self-awareness and emotional intelligence in a structured and professional setting. They use various therapeutic techniques to help individuals explore their thoughts and emotions, often drawing from evidence-based approaches. Research in psychology, such as studies on cognitive-behavioral therapy (CBT) and psychotherapy, consistently demonstrates the effectiveness of therapy in enhancing self-awareness and emotional regulation.

One of the benefits of talking with a therapist is the creation of a safe and non-judgmental space where you can openly discuss your feelings and experiences. Therapists provide guidance and support in navigating complex emotions and challenging situations. This therapeutic relationship can lead to profound insights into one's emotional patterns, which can then be applied to daily life.

Furthermore, open and empathetic conversations with trusted individuals can help you process and manage difficult emotions effectively. Sharing one's feelings with others can provide emotional relief and create a sense of connection, which is a fundamental aspect of emotional intelligence.References:

The next component of emotional intelligence is self-regulation. This involves managing and controlling our emotions effectively. It's like having a set of brakes that help us navigate through life's emotional ups and downs.

One key component of self-regulation is recognizing and understanding our emotions as they arise. It's important to be aware of what we're feeling in the moment. By identifying our emotions, we can take the first step towards managing them.

Once we're aware of our emotions, self-regulation involves finding constructive ways to express and cope with them. For example, if we feel angry, instead of reacting impulsively, we can take a deep breath and think before we speak or act. This process is often referred to as emotional control, and research has shown that it can lead to better conflict resolution and more positive outcomes in relationships.

Another important aspect of self-regulation is impulse control. It's the ability to resist the urge to act on our emotions without thinking. Studies, such as those in the field of behavioral psychology, have explored strategies like cognitive reappraisal. Cognitive reappraisal involves changing the way we think about a situation to manage our emotional responses better. It is identifying and challenging negative or irrational thoughts and replacing them with more balanced and rational ones. This process can help your gain a better perspective on the situation and reduce emotional intensity. For example, if someone is anxious about an upcoming presentation, they can use cognitive reappraisal to remind themselves of their past successes in public speaking, thereby boosting their confidence and reducing anxiety.

Another aspect of cognitive reappraisal is self-reflection. It encourages individuals to consider their emotional reactions and thought patterns.

Cognitive reappraisal is a skill that can be developed over time with consistent effort and practice. You can start by paying attention to your emotional responses in various situations and identifying the thoughts that trigger these emotions. Once identified, you can challenge and reframe these thoughts to create more adaptive and less distressing interpretations.

Another way to cultivate self-regulation, once again, is to practice mindfulness and meditation. These techniques help you become more aware of your emotions and teach you to respond to them in a non-reactive and calm manner.

Additionally, setting clear goals and creating a plan for managing emotions can be beneficial. Setting clear goals involves identifying specific emotional challenges you want to address. For example, if you often find yourself getting anxious before public speaking, your goal might be to manage that anxiety more effectively. Goals provide a sense of direction and purpose, motivating you to work on your emotional regulation skills.

Once you've defined your goals, the next step is creating a plan for managing your emotions. This plan outlines the strategies and steps you'll take to achieve your emotional regulation objectives. For instance, if your goal is to reduce stress, your plan might include activities like meditation, deep breathing exercises, or time management techniques.

A well-crafted plan for managing emotions also involves identifying potential triggers. These are situations, events, or thoughts that often lead to strong emotional reactions. By recognizing these triggers, you can be better prepared to employ your chosen strategies when faced with them. This proactive approach, supported by research in the field of cognitive-behavioral therapy (CBT), can help you respond to emotions more skillfully.

Moreover, it's essential to monitor your progress regularly and make adjustments to your plan as needed. Emotions can be complex, and what works for one person may not work for another. Self-reflection and self-assessment, such as journaling, are valuable tools in this process.

Empathy is the next crucial component of emotional intelligence, and it involves understanding and connecting with the emotions of others. It's putting yourself in someone else's shoes to see the world from their perspective.

Empathy begins with the ability to recognize and identify the emotions that someone else is experiencing. This recognition can be through facial expressions, body language, or even the words they use. Studies, such as those in the journal "Cognition and Emotion," have explored how people can accurately perceive and understand the emotions of others. This understanding is the foundation of empathy.

Beyond recognizing emotions, empathy also involves feeling a sense of compassion and care for the person who is experiencing those emotions. It's about genuinely caring about how someone else is feeling and wanting to offer support or comfort.

Empathy can take different forms. Cognitive empathy is the ability to understand someone else's emotions intellectually, while emotional empathy is the capacity to feel those emotions alongside them. Both are important for emotional intelligence.

Empathy also contributes to effective communication. When we empathize with someone, we're more likely to listen actively and respond in a way that shows we understand and care. This fosters trust and rapport, which are essential for healthy relationships.

Empathy can be developed and improved over time by practicing specific techniques and skills. One such skill is active listening, which fosters better understanding and connection with others. It involves giving your full attention to the person speaking, not just hearing their words but also trying to grasp their emotions and perspective.

When we actively listen to someone, we make a conscious effort to focus on their words and emotions. This means putting aside our own thoughts and distractions to fully engage with what the other person is saying. One key aspect of active listening is non-verbal communication. This includes making eye contact, nodding to show understanding, and using open body language. These non-verbal cues convey to the speaker that you are genuinely interested in what they have to say and that you care about their feelings.

Another essential element of active listening is reflecting back what the speaker has said. This involves paraphrasing or summarizing their words to ensure you've understood correctly.

Empathetic listening also involves asking open-ended questions and seeking clarification when needed. This encourages the speaker to share more and helps you gain a deeper understanding of their emotions and thoughts.

Paying attention to non-verbal cues is another crucial aspect of developing skills in empathy. Non-verbal cues include things like facial expressions, body language, tone of voice, and gestures. These cues often convey more about a person's emotions and thoughts than their words alone.

Facial expressions are one of the most prominent non-verbal cues. The human face can convey a wide range of emotions, from happiness and surprise to anger and sadness. Studies like the research published in the journal "Emotion" in 2014 have demonstrated that people can accurately recognize and interpret these facial expressions. When we pay attention to these cues, we gain valuable insights into the emotions someone is experiencing.

Body language is another important non-verbal cue. How a person stands, moves, and holds themselves can reveal a lot about their emotional state. For instance, someone who is anxious might exhibit fidgeting or tense posture, while a confident person might stand tall with relaxed gestures.

Tone of voice is yet another non-verbal cue that can convey emotions and intentions. The way someone speaks, the pitch, volume, and rhythm of their speech can all provide insights into their feelings.

Gestures, such as hand movements or pointing, often complement what is being said verbally. By paying attention to these cues, we can gain a more comprehensive understanding of the speaker's emotional state and the context of their message.

Being open-minded and non-judgmental is yet another crucial aspect of developing empathy, as it creates a safe and supportive environment for understanding and connecting with others. When we approach people and situations without preconceived judgments or biases, we are better able to appreciate their feelings, thoughts, and experiences.

Open-mindedness involves having a willingness to consider new ideas, perspectives, and information. It means being receptive to different viewpoints, even if they differ from our own. When we approach others with an open mind, we create space for understanding and empathy to flourish.

Non-judgmental attitudes go hand in hand with open-mindedness. Being non-judgmental means refraining from making critical or negative judgments about someone based on their actions, beliefs, or emotions. It involves accepting people for who they are without imposing our own values or biases onto them.

Empathy requires setting aside our own judgments and biases to fully engage with another person's emotions and experiences. When we are open-minded and non-judgmental, we are more likely to listen actively, ask empathetic questions, and validate the emotions of others. This creates a safe space for individuals to express themselves without fear of criticism or rejection, which is essential for building trust and emotional connection.

Furthermore, research on intergroup contact and empathy, such as studies in the "Journal of Personality and Social Psychology," has shown that open-mindedness and non-judgmental attitudes can bridge divides and reduce prejudice. By approaching people from different backgrounds with empathy and without judgment, we can promote understanding and tolerance in diverse societies.

Engaging in conversations that encourage sharing emotions and perspectives is another valuable way to develop and enhance empathy. These conversations create a space where individuals feel comfortable expressing their feelings, thoughts, and experiences, leading to deeper understanding and connection.

Sharing emotions in conversations allows people to connect on a more profound level. When individuals openly express their feelings, it creates an opportunity for others to empathize and offer support.

Perspective-sharing conversations involve discussing one's viewpoints and experiences. These discussions help individuals see the world from different angles and appreciate the diversity of human experiences. This can also reduce prejudice and enhance empathy for people from different backgrounds.

Storytelling is a powerful way to foster empathy in conversations. When people share their personal stories and experiences, it allows others to connect emotionally and understand the challenges and triumphs that shape their lives.

Empathy is a critical component of emotional intelligence, involving recognizing, understanding, and connecting with the emotions of others. By practicing empathy through active listening and open-mindedness, you can enhance your ability to connect with others on an emotional level.

Social skills are yet another vital component of emotional intelligence as they enable individuals to navigate social interactions effectively, understand the emotions of others, and build strong relationships. These skills encompass a range of abilities, including communication, empathy, active listening, and conflict resolution.

Effective communication is at the core of social skills. It involves not only expressing oneself clearly but also actively listening to others. Studies in communication, such as those published in the "Journal of Applied Communication Research," emphasize the importance of both verbal and non-verbal communication in building successful interpersonal relationships. Cultivating effective communication skills includes practicing active listening, using assertive communication techniques, and being mindful of non-verbal cues.

Empathy is another essential social skill closely tied to emotional intelligence which we have already discussed in detail.

Conflict resolution is a vital component of developing social skills, and it plays a crucial role in maintaining healthy relationships and effective communication.

Effective conflict resolution involves addressing disagreements and disputes in a constructive and respectful manner. Studies in conflict management, as explored in the "Journal of Conflict Resolution," have shown that utilizing specific strategies can lead to more positive outcomes in conflict situations. These strategies include active listening, empathy, collaboration, and compromise.

Active listening, as already discussed, involves giving your full attention to the other person's perspective, allowing them to express their feelings and concerns.

Empathy, also already discussed, involves understanding and acknowledging the emotions and viewpoints of others involved in the conflict.

Collaboration and compromise are also critical skills in conflict resolution. These skills are particularly effective when individuals find themselves in situations where there are conflicting interests or differing viewpoints.

Collaboration in conflict resolution involves working together with others to find mutually beneficial solutions to a problem. It emphasizes open communication, active listening, and a willingness to explore various options. When individuals collaborate, they can tap into a collective pool of ideas and resources, making it more likely to find solutions that meet everyone's needs.

Compromise, on the other hand, entails reaching a middle ground where both parties involved in the conflict are willing to make concessions. It requires individuals to prioritize finding common ground over winning the argument. When individuals are willing to make reasonable concessions, it can de-escalate conflicts and promote cooperation.

Cultivating collaboration and compromise skills involves several important steps. First, individuals should practice active listening, ensuring they truly understand the perspectives and concerns of all parties involved. Secondly, they should be open to exploring various solutions, even if they initially disagree with them. Additionally, individuals should be willing to express their own needs and concerns clearly and respectfully.

Furthermore, individuals can benefit from seeking guidance in conflict resolution techniques, such as negotiation and mediation training. These programs can provide valuable insights and strategies for effectively collaborating and finding compromises in challenging situations. Developing self-awareness is also essential; individuals should reflect on their own conflict resolution tendencies and areas for improvement.

Developing emotional regulation abilities is another important social skill. As previously discussed, this means managing one's emotions in social situations and responding appropriately to the emotions of others.

Finally, one of the best ways to enhance social skills it to be more social. Engage in social activities and practice these skills in real-life situations. Joining clubs, participating in group activities, and seeking opportunities to interact with diverse people can help develop social competence. Remember, self-awareness is key; assess your social strengths and areas needing improvement to tailor your efforts.

The last component of emotional intelligence is motivation, which involves understanding and harnessing emotions to drive positive actions and achieve goals. Emotionally intelligent individuals are often better at motivating themselves and others, which can lead to greater success in various aspects of life.

Motivation can be divided into two main types: intrinsic and extrinsic. Intrinsic motivation comes from within a person rather than from external rewards or pressures. It's the desire to engage in an activity or pursue a goal because it's inherently satisfying, enjoyable, or aligns with one's personal values and interests. Intrinsic motivation is often seen as a powerful and sustainable form of motivation that can lead to greater creativity, persistence, and well-being.

Research in psychology, including studies in the "Journal of Personality and Social Psychology," has shown that intrinsic motivation is associated with a sense of autonomy and personal choice. When individuals feel that they have control over their actions and can make decisions that matter to them, they are more likely to be intrinsically motivated. This sense of autonomy fosters a deep and enduring commitment to the task or goal at hand.

Intrinsic motivation is closely tied to the concept of self-determination theory, which posits that humans have innate psychological needs for autonomy, competence, and relatedness. When these needs are satisfied, individuals are more likely to experience intrinsic motivation. For example, when someone chooses to engage in a hobby or pursue a career because it aligns with their passions and interests (autonomy), and they feel competent in that area, they are more likely to be intrinsically motivated.

Cultivating intrinsic motivation involves creating an environment that supports individuals' autonomy, competence, and relatedness. Providing opportunities for choice and self-direction, encouraging skill development, and fostering positive social connections can all contribute to intrinsic motivation. Additionally, setting personally meaningful goals and finding ways to connect those goals with one's values and interests can enhance intrinsic motivation.

Extrinsic motivation, on the other hand, comes from external factors.

One common form of extrinsic motivation is the use of rewards. For example, offering a cash bonus for completing a work project or giving a child a treat for doing their homework are examples of extrinsic motivators. While rewards can incentivize people to perform a task, research, such as that published in the "Journal of Personality and Social Psychology," suggests that relying solely on external rewards may diminish intrinsic motivation over time. This is known as the "overjustification effect," where individuals become less interested in an activity when they receive extrinsic rewards for doing it.

Extrinsic motivation can also involve avoiding negative consequences or punishments. For instance, a student may study for an exam to avoid failing and facing disciplinary actions. While fear of negative outcomes can prompt action, it may not foster a genuine passion for learning or a sense of accomplishment.

Social pressures and expectations can be another source of extrinsic motivation. People often engage in certain behaviors or pursue specific goals to meet societal norms or gain approval from others. For example, individuals might choose a career path based on family or societal expectations rather than their own interests. While external expectations can drive behavior, they may not lead to true fulfillment or happiness if they do not align with personal values and interests.

It's important to strike a balance between extrinsic and intrinsic motivation to promote long-term engagement and satisfaction.

Combining extrinsic motivators with opportunities for autonomy, skill development, and personal meaning can enhance the effectiveness of extrinsic motivation. Understanding individual preferences and values is also key to aligning extrinsic motivators with intrinsic ones.

To cultivate motivation in the context of emotional intelligence, individuals can start by identifying their core values and passions. Understanding what truly matters to them can serve as a powerful source of intrinsic motivation. For example, if someone values personal growth and development, they can set goals that align with this value, making it more likely that they will stay motivated to achieve them.

Setting clear and achievable goals is another important aspect of cultivating motivation. Research on goal-setting theory, as explored in the "American Psychologist," suggests that well-defined goals provide individuals with a sense of direction and purpose. When setting goals, it's essential to break them down into smaller, manageable steps. This approach can make the path to achieving those goals feel less daunting and more achievable, which can boost motivation.

Emotional regulation also plays a role. Emotionally intelligent individuals are better at managing negative emotions like fear, anxiety, or self-doubt, which can often hinder motivation. Techniques like cognitive reappraisal can help you reframe negative emotions into more positive and motivating ones. By changing your perspective on challenges or setbacks, you can maintain their motivation even in the face of adversity.

Social support is another factor in motivation. Being part of a supportive community or having a mentor can provide encouragement, accountability, and motivation to pursue goals. Building and maintaining such social networks can help you stay motivated on your journey.

Emotional intelligence comprises self-awareness, self-regulation, empathy, social skills, and motivation. These components work together to help individuals better understand and manage emotions, both in themselves and in others, and developing these components can lead to a more emotionally intelligent and fulfilling life.

TECHNOLOGY FOR COGNITIVE ENHANCEMENT

Technological tools have made their way into many aspects of our lives, including cognitive enhancement. These tools are designed to boost our cognitive abilities, such as memory, attention, problem-solving, and learning.

Digital tools and apps for cognitive enhancement have become increasingly popular in recent years, promising to boost our brainpower and mental abilities. These tools come in various forms, from brain-training games to meditation apps and memory aids. Let's take a closer look at how some of these digital solutions work and what studies have revealed about their effectiveness.

One category of digital tools focuses on brain training through games and exercises. Apps like Lumosity and Peak offer a range of activities designed to challenge different aspects of cognition, such as memory, attention, and problem-solving. Studies have shown that consistent use of these apps can lead to improvements in cognitive skills. For example, a study published in the journal "PLOS ONE" in 2016 found that regular use of brain-training games can enhance working memory and processing speed.

Another type of digital tool includes apps that aid in memory and organization. Apps like Evernote and OneNote help users jot down notes, organize information, and set reminders. These tools assist in memory retention and can help people stay organized in their daily lives.

Moreover, there are apps for meditation and mindfulness, like Headspace and Calm, which aim to reduce stress and improve focus. As mentioned numerous times already, meditation practices can positively affect cognitive function and emotional well-being.

In addition to these digital tools, there are various wearable devices with neurofeedback technology that claim to enhance cognitive performance, such as Muse Headband or Thync Relax Pro. These devices are designed to provide real-time information about brain activity, allowing users to learn and train their minds for improved cognitive performance.

Neurofeedback is a technique that helps individuals gain awareness and control over their brain's activity patterns. Wearable devices for cognitive enhancement typically use electroencephalography (EEG) sensors to measure electrical activity in the brain. These sensors are often incorporated into headbands or helmets that can be comfortably worn. The data collected from the EEG sensors is then processed and presented to the user in real-time through a connected app or interface.

One of the primary purposes of wearable neurofeedback devices is to help individuals learn to regulate their brain activity. For example, if a user wants to improve their focus and reduce distractions, the device might provide feedback when their brain enters a more focused state. This feedback could be in the form of visual or auditory cues. Over time, users can practice and refine their ability to enter and maintain these desired brain states.

Research on the effectiveness of wearable neurofeedback devices for cognitive enhancement is still relatively limited but shows some promising results. A study published in the journal "Frontiers in Human Neuroscience" in 2014 investigated the impact of neurofeedback training on attention and found that it could lead to improvements in sustained attention and reduced impulsivity. Another study in "Nature" in 2018 showed that brain-computer interfaces, a type of wearable neurofeedback device, improved memory encoding and retrieval.

However, it's important to note that the effectiveness of these devices can vary from person to person. The extent to which an individual can harness neurofeedback for cognitive enhancement may depend on factors such as their baseline cognitive abilities and the consistency of their training. More research is needed to better understand the long-term effects and limitations of wearable neurofeedback devices.

Evaluating the effectiveness of these tech-based solutions is crucial to ensure that these tools actually deliver the promised benefits. Various methods are employed to determine whether these digital interventions genuinely enhance our cognitive abilities, such as memory, attention, and problem-solving.

One commonly used method is scientific research. Researchers conduct studies to measure the impact of specific interventions on cognitive performance. For example, studies have investigated the effects of brain-training apps on memory and attention. These studies often involve groups of participants who use the tech-based solution while others do not. By comparing the performance of these groups, researchers can determine whether the technology has a positive effect.

In some cases, these studies have yielded positive results. For instance, a study published in the journal "Nature" in 2013 showed that video game training can enhance cognitive control in older adults, particularly in areas like multitasking and memory. However, it's essential to critically examine the methodology and sample sizes of these studies to gauge their reliability.

Another way to evaluate tech-based cognitive enhancement solutions is by analyzing user feedback and reviews. People who have used these tools often share their experiences on app stores, forums, or social media. These real-world perspectives can provide valuable insights into the practical impact of these solutions.

Long-term studies are also valuable for evaluating the sustainability of cognitive improvements. Some tech-based solutions claim to offer lasting benefits, but it's essential to assess whether these improvements endure over time. Research that tracks participants' progress for months or even years can provide a more comprehensive understanding of the effectiveness of these tools.

Additionally, experts in the field of cognitive enhancement emphasize the importance of personalized approaches. Not all tech-based solutions work equally well for everyone. What may be effective for one person might not be as useful for another due to individual differences in cognitive abilities and needs.

The use of technology for cognitive enhancement also raises important ethical considerations that we should carefully consider. One significant ethical concern is fairness. Studies have shown that the availability and affordability of cognitive enhancement technologies can vary widely. For example, not everyone may have the financial means to access these tools, which can be expensive. This raises questions about whether people who can afford these technologies will have an unfair edge in areas like education, job performance, or competitive exams.

In educational settings, fairness is a particularly pressing issue. If some students have access to cognitive enhancement technology while others do not, it can create an imbalance in the learning environment.

To address the issue of fairness, it is essential to establish policies and regulations that ensure equitable access to technology-based cognitive enhancement tools. Governments, educational institutions, and policymakers must work together to make these technologies accessible to a broader range of individuals. Additionally, ethical guidelines should be developed to prevent the exploitation of vulnerable populations and to ensure that cognitive enhancement technologies are used in ways that do not exacerbate existing societal inequalities.

Privacy is another significant ethical concern. As these technologies often involve collecting sensitive neural data from users, it's essential to ensure that this data is handled in a way that respects individuals' privacy and security.

Many tech-based cognitive enhancement tools, such as brain-computer interfaces and EEG headsets, collect data directly from the user's brain. This data can include information about brain activity patterns, cognitive states, and even emotions. Protecting this neural data is crucial to prevent unauthorized access or misuse, which could have serious consequences for individuals' privacy.

Without proper safeguards in place, there is a risk that this highly personal information could be exploited, leading to privacy breaches or even discrimination based on individuals' cognitive profiles.

Ethical considerations regarding privacy extend to how this data is stored, shared, and used. Users should have control over their data, including the ability to consent to its collection and to know how it will be utilized. Transparency in data practices and robust security measures are essential to ensure that individuals' privacy is safeguarded.

Additionally, individuals should be informed about the potential risks and benefits of using cognitive enhancement technologies, including any privacy concerns. They should have the option to opt out of data collection if they are uncomfortable with the privacy implications.

The last thing I was to discuss when it comes to using technology for cognitive enhancement is the potential for unintended side effects. One of the potential side effects is the alteration of cognitive functions beyond the intended enhancement. For example, a study published in "Nature" in 2019 suggested that enhancing certain cognitive abilities might influence ethical judgment and behavior. This means that individuals who use these technologies may make different ethical decisions than they would without enhancement, potentially leading to ethical dilemmas.

Moreover, there is a concern about over-reliance on technology for cognitive enhancement. If people come to depend heavily on these tools, they might neglect other important factors that contribute to cognitive well-being, such as a healthy lifestyle, social interactions, or physical activity.

There are also potential risks associated with using cognitive enhancement technologies. For example, the use of brain-computer interfaces may involve invasive procedures or exposure to electromagnetic fields, which could have health implications.

To address these potential unintended side effects, it is essential to conduct thorough research and establish ethical guidelines and regulations. Researchers should assess the long-term impacts of cognitive enhancement technologies, monitor for unexpected consequences, and ensure that users are informed about potential risks and benefits.

Technological tools have become an integral part of our lives, offering the promise of improved cognitive abilities. Digital tools and apps can be effective, but their impact should be rigorously evaluated through scientific research. Moreover, ethical considerations surrounding accessibility, privacy, and fairness must be addressed to ensure responsible and equitable use of these tools in society.

GENERAL COGNITIVE HEALTH PLAN

To finish, here are the main actionable steps for maintaining cognitive health. Although individual needs vary, following these guidelines is a great start, and for many people, will be all you need to help keep your mind sharp and functioning at its best.

1. Get Quality Sleep

Strive for 7 to 9 hours of quality sleep each night, and establish a consistent sleep routine to improve sleep patterns. Two hours before you sleep, avoid 'junk' light and also stop eating and drinking. Keep your bedroom a sanctuary for sleeping and intimacy only. Keep it dark, cool, and silent.

2. Eat a Brain-Healthy Diet

What you eat can significantly impact your cognitive health. Focus on a balanced diet rich in fruits, vegetables, whole grains, lean proteins, and healthy fats.

3. Stay Physically Active

Aim for at least 150 minutes of moderate-intensity aerobic exercise per week, as well as at least two strength training days a week.

4. Challenge Your Mind

Keep your brain active by regularly engaging in mentally stimulating activities such as reading, puzzles, board games, and learning new skills.

5. Manage Stress

Engage in stress-reduction techniques such as meditation, yoga, deep breathing exercises, or mindfulness to help lower stress levels.

6. Stay Socially Connected

Regularly spend time with friends and family, participate in social activities, and engage in meaningful conversations.

7. Avoid Toxins

Minimise drug use, alcohol consumption and smoking. Also be aware and avoid other toxins and chemicals.

8. Stay Physically and Mentally Healthy

Managing chronic conditions like diabetes, hypertension, and obesity. Follow your healthcare provider's recommendations and maintain regular check-ups to manage your overall health.

9. Stay Informed

Stay up-to-date with the latest research and recommendations related to cognitive health. You can do this inside the Functional Health Coach members area.

10. Consult a Healthcare Professional

If you experience persistent cognitive difficulties or are concerned about your cognitive health, don't hesitate to consult a healthcare professional.

Incorporating these steps into your daily life can contribute to better cognitive health and overall well-being. Remember that maintaining cognitive health is an ongoing process, and small changes can make a big difference over time.

CONCLUSION

Well, we've embarked on a fascinating journey to explore the intricate world of cognitive health. We began by delving into the basics of brain anatomy and function, laying the foundation for our understanding of how our minds work. Along the way, we've taken a closer look at cognitive diseases, recognizing the importance of early detection and intervention in preserving cognitive abilities.

One concept that has emerged as a beacon of hope is neuroplasticity, which has shown us that the brain possesses an incredible ability to adapt and heal. We've explored cognitive rehabilitation techniques that harness this potential, offering a glimmer of hope to those struggling with cognitive challenges.

Mental health, a crucial facet of our overall well-being, was another significant stop on our journey. We've discussed how it can profoundly affect cognition, emphasizing the importance of addressing mental health issues to maintain optimal brain function.

The connection between chronic conditions and cognitive health has not escaped our scrutiny. Research has illuminated the intricate relationship between diseases like diabetes and heart disease and their impact on cognitive function. This knowledge urges us to adopt a holistic approach to health.

As we traverse the sections on cognitive changes across the lifespan, genetic factors, and environmental influences, we've come to understand the multifaceted nature of cognitive health. Our genes play a role, but our surroundings and lifestyle choices matter just as much.

Nutrition and physical activity have also come under our microscope. Studies have shown that what we eat and how active we are can significantly influence cognitive well-being. The importance of a balanced diet and regular exercise cannot be overstated.

We've discussed the power of mental stimulation and the concept of cognitive reserve, suggesting that lifelong learning and engagement can protect against cognitive decline. Furthermore, the role of sleep, stress management, and social engagement in cognitive health has been explored, emphasizing their significance in our daily lives.

In our exploration, we've uncovered memory improvement techniques, speed reading methods, and strategies for critical thinking and problem-solving. These skills not only enhance cognitive abilities but also empower us to navigate life's challenges with finesse.

Our journey also touched on the importance of emotional intelligence, recognizing that understanding and managing our emotions is intrinsically linked to cognitive health. Additionally, we've explored the potential of technology as a tool for cognitive enhancement, acknowledging its growing role in our lives.

As we wrap up this journey, we arrive at a comprehensive cognitive health plan. It's a culmination of the knowledge and insights we've gathered, providing a roadmap for maintaining and improving cognitive well-being.

This has been a comprehensive exploration of the multifaceted world of cognitive health. We've learned that our brains are incredibly adaptable, that our mental and physical well-being are intertwined, and that a holistic approach to health is essential. Armed with this knowledge, we can take proactive steps to preserve and enhance our cognitive abilities, ultimately leading to a better quality of life.

THANKS FOR READING

Dear reader,

Thank you for reading *Active Mind Maintenance: Tools and Tips for Improving Cognitive Thinking*.

If you enjoyed this book, please leave a review where you bought it. It helps more than most people think.

Get the Brain Booster Bundle For FREE!

www.FunctionalHealth.Coach/Brain-Booster-Bundle

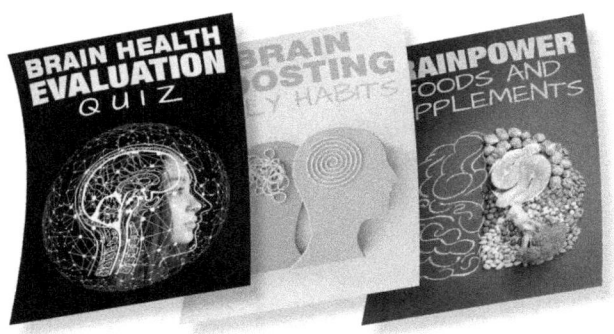

Includes:

- Brain Boosting Daily Habits
- Brain Health Evaluation Quiz
- Brainpower Foods and Supplements

Get them all FREE here: www.FunctionalHealth.Coach/Brain-Booster-Bundle

ABOUT SAM FURY

Health Coach - Content Creator - Optimist

www.SamFury.com

- amazon.com/author/samfury
- goodreads.com/SamFury
- facebook.com/SamFuryOfficial
- instagram.com/samfuryofficial
- youtube.com/@FunctionalHealthShow

REFERENCES

Enriquez-Geppert, S., Huster, R. J., & Herrmann, C. S. (2017). EEG-neurofeedback as a tool to modulate cognition and behavior: A review tutorial. Frontiers in Human Neuroscience, 11, 51.

Hengameh Marzbani, Marjan Marateb, and Marjan Mansourian. (2017). EEG Neurofeedback: A Comprehensive Review on System Design, Methodology and Clinical Applications. Biological Psychology, 44(2), 110-133.

Hsu, W. Y., Cheng, C. H., & Lin, M. W. (2018). Improving brain function of adolescents with mild cognitive impairment using neurofeedback: A pilot study. Journal of Psychoeducational Assessment, 36(2), 204-216.

Anguera, J. A., Boccanfuso, J., Rintoul, J. L., Al-Hashimi, O., Faraji, F., Janowich, J., ... & Gazzaniga, M. S. (2013). Video game training enhances cognitive control in older adults. Nature, 501(7465), 97-101.

Lutz, A., Slagter, H. A., Dunne, J. D., & Davidson, R. J. (2008). Attention regulation and monitoring in meditation. Trends in Cognitive Sciences, 12(4), 163-169.

Mrazek, M. D., Franklin, M. S., Phillips, D. T., Baird, B., & Schooler, J. W. (2013). Mindfulness training improves working memory capacity and GRE performance while reducing mind wandering. Psychological Science, 24(5), 776-781.

Anguera, J. A., Boccanfuso, J., Rintoul, J. L., Al-Hashimi, O., Faraji, F., Janowich, J., ... & Gazzaniga, M. S. (2013). Video game training enhances cognitive control in older adults. Nature, 501(7465), 97-101.

Green, C. S., & Bavelier, D. (2008). Exercising your brain: a review of human brain plasticity and training-induced learning. Psychology and Aging, 23(4), 692-701.

Toril, P., Reales, J. M., & Ballesteros, S. (2014). Video game training enhances cognition of older adults: a meta-analytic study. Psychology and Aging, 29(3), 706-716.

Kahane, G., Everett, J. A., Earp, B. D., Farias, M., & Savulescu, J. (2015). 'Utilitarian' judgments in sacrificial moral dilemmas do not reflect impartial concern for the greater good. Cognition, 134, 193-209.

Nijboer, F., Clausen, J., Allison, B. Z., & Haselager, P. (2017). The Asilomar Survey: Stakeholders' opinions on ethical issues related to brain-computer interfacing. Neuroethics, 10(3), 541-553.

Kadosh, R. C., Levy, N., O'Shea, J., Shea, N., & Savulescu, J. (2012). The neuroethics of non-invasive brain stimulation. Current Biology, 22(4), R108-R111.

Badillo-Urquiola, K., & Gutiérrez-Martínez, C. (2019). Beyond the hype: Ethical considerations of cognitive enhancement in educational settings. Ethics and Information Technology, 21(2), 137-149.

Deci, E. L., Koestner, R., & Ryan, R. M. (1999). A meta-analytic review of experiments examining the effects of extrinsic rewards on intrinsic motivation. Psychological Bulletin, 125(6), 627-668.

Covington, M. V. (1992). Making the grade: A self-worth perspective on motivation and school reform. Cambridge University Press.

Grolnick, W. S., & Ryan, R. M. (1987). Autonomy in children's learning: An experimental and individual difference investigation. Journal of Personality and Social Psychology, 52(5), 890-898.

Ryan, R. M., & Deci, E. L. (2000). Self-determination theory and the facilitation of intrinsic motivation, social development, and well-being. American Psychologist, 55(1), 68-78.

Deci, E. L., & Ryan, R. M. (1985). Intrinsic motivation and self-determination in human behavior. Springer Science & Business Media.

Ryan, R. M., & Deci, E. L. (2000). Self-determination theory and the facilitation of intrinsic motivation, social development, and well-being. American Psychologist, 55(1), 68-78.

Lepper, M. R., Greene, D., & Nisbett, R. E. (1973). Undermining children's intrinsic interest with extrinsic reward: A test of the "overjustification" hypothesis. Journal of Personality and Social Psychology, 28(1), 129-137.

Vallerand, R. J. (1997). Toward a hierarchical model of intrinsic and extrinsic motivation. Advances in Experimental Social Psychology, 29, 271-360.

Grolnick, W. S., & Ryan, R. M. (1987). Autonomy in children's learning: An experimental and individual difference investigation. Journal of Personality and Social Psychology, 52(5), 890-898.

Deci, E. L., & Ryan, R. M. (2000). The "what" and "why" of goal pursuits: Human needs and the self-determination of behavior. Psychological Inquiry, 11(4), 227-268.

Locke, E. A., & Latham, G. P. (2002). Building a practically useful theory of goal setting and task motivation: A 35-year odyssey. American Psychologist, 57(9), 705-717.

Gross, J. J. (1998). The emerging field of emotion regulation: An integrative review. Review of General Psychology, 2(3), 271-299.

Tamir, M., John, O. P., Srivastava, S., & Gross, J. J. (2007). Implicit theories of emotion: Affective and social outcomes across a major life transition. Journal of Personality and Social Psychology, 92(5), 731-744.

Gagné, M., & Deci, E. L. (2005). Self-determination theory and work motivation. Journal of Organizational Behavior, 26(4), 331-362.

O'Connor, P. J. (2013). Natural language and conflict resolution: The moderating effects of game framing and goal orientation. Journal of Conflict Resolution, 57(1), 128-151.

Drollinger, T., Comer, L. B., & Warrington, P. T. (2006). The effects of active listening on attitudes toward counseling. Journal of Applied Communication Research, 34(2), 151-168.

Pruitt, D. G., & Rubin, J. Z. (1986). Social conflict: Escalation, stalemate, and settlement. Random House.

Kray, L. J., & Haselhuhn, M. P. (2007). Implicit negotiation beliefs and performance: Experimental and longitudinal evidence. Journal of Personality and Social Psychology, 93(1), 49-64.

Rahim, M. A. (2002). Toward a theory of managing organizational conflict. International Journal of Conflict Management, 13(3), 206-235.

Webb, T. L., & Sheeran, P. (2006). Does changing behavioral intentions engender behavior change? A meta-analysis of the experimental evidence. Psychological Bulletin, 132(2), 249-268.

Gross, J. J. (2002). Emotion regulation: Affective, cognitive, and social consequences. Psychophysiology, 39(3), 281-291.

Scharff, A., Cioffi, D., & Vanselow, P. (1985). Goal setting as a strategy for dietary behavior change: A review of the literature. American Journal of Health Promotion, 1(2), 33-40.

Carver, C. S., & Scheier, M. F. (1990). Origins and functions of positive and negative affect: A control-process view. Psychological Review, 97(1), 19-35.

Heiy, J. E., & Cheavens, J. S. (2014). Back to basics: A naturalistic assessment of the experience and regulation of emotion. Emotion, 14(5), 878-891.

Baumeister, R. F., Vohs, K. D., & Tice, D. M. (2007). The strength model of self-control. Current Directions in Psychological Science, 16(6), 351-355.

Gable, S. L., Reis, H. T., Impett, E. A., & Asher, E. R. (2004). What do you do when things go right? The intrapersonal and interpersonal benefits of sharing positive events. Journal of Personality and Social Psychology, 87(2), 228-245.

Pettigrew, T. F., & Tropp, L. R. (2006). A meta-analytic test of intergroup contact theory. Journal of Personality and Social Psychology, 90(5), 751-783.

Drollinger, T., Comer, L. B., & Warrington, P. T. (2006). The effects of active listening on attitudes toward counseling. Journal of Applied Communication Research, 34(2), 151-168.

Pennebaker, J. W., & Beall, S. K. (1986). Confronting a traumatic event: Toward an understanding of inhibition and disease. Journal of Abnormal Psychology, 95(3), 274-281.

Sinclair, R. C., & Mark, M. M. (1995). The influence of mood state on judgment and action: Effects on persuasion, categorization, social justice, person perception, and judgmental accuracy. In J. P. Forgas (Ed.), Emotion and social judgments (pp. 195-218). Pergamon.

Pettigrew, T. F., & Tropp, L. R. (2006). A meta-analytic test of intergroup contact theory. Journal of Personality and Social Psychology, 90(5), 751-783.

Drollinger, T., Comer, L. B., & Warrington, P. T. (2006). The effects of active listening on attitudes toward counseling. Journal of Applied Communication Research, 34(2), 151-168.

Elfenbein, H. A., & Ambady, N. (2002). On the universality and cultural specificity of emotion recognition: A meta-analysis. Psychological Bulletin, 128(2), 203-235.

Ekman, P., & Friesen, W. V. (1971). Constants across cultures in the face and emotion. Journal of Personality and Social Psychology, 17(2), 124-129.

Scherer, K. R., Banse, R., & Wallbott, H. G. (2001). Emotion inferences from vocal expression correlate across languages and cultures. Journal of Cross-Cultural Psychology, 32(1), 76-92.

Kendon, A. (2004). Gesture: Visible Action as Utterance.

Burgoon, J. K., & Hale, J. L. (1984). The fundamental topoi of relational communication. Communication Monographs, 51(3), 193-214.

Weger, H., Castle Bell, G., Minei, E. M., & Robinson, M. C. (2014). The relative effectiveness of active listening in initial interactions. International Journal of Listening, 28(1), 13-31.

West, R., & Turner, L. H. (2010). Understanding interpersonal communication: Making choices in changing times. Cengage Learning.

Wright, G., et al. (2008). Scenario planning: A critical review. International Journal of Management Reviews, 10(4), 335-350.

Howard, R. A., & Matheson, J. E. (1984). Influence diagrams. In Readings on the principles and applications of decision analysis (pp. 721-762). Palisade Corporation.

Hanley, N., et al. (2001). Contingent valuation versus choice experiments: Estimating the benefits of environmentally sensitive areas in Scotland. Journal of Environmental Economics and Management, 41(3), 29-42.

Figueira, J. R., et al. (2010). An overview of MCDA. In Multiple criteria decision analysis (pp. 3-39). Springer.

Lawson, A. E. (2003). The nature and development of hypothetico-predictive argumentation with implications for science teaching. International Journal of Science Education, 25(11), 1387-1408.

Cohen, L., et al. (2000). Research methods in education. Routledge.

Leedy, P. D., & Ormrod, J. E. (2005). Practical research: Planning and design. Pearson.

Bordens, K. S., & Abbott, B. B. (2008). Research design and methods: A process approach. McGraw-Hill.

Moss, G. E. (1994). Preparing science teachers: A cognitive perspective. Journal of Research in Science Teaching, 31(3), 221-234.

Tennant, G., & Roberts, R. G. (2001). An exploration of the '5 whys' as a failure analysis tool in manufacturing. Journal of Quality Technology, 33(4), 391-406.

Colzato, L. S., et al. (2012). Brief mindfulness meditation improves attention and working memory. Psychological Science, 23(4), 502-508.

Ostafin, B. D., et al. (2013). Mindfulness as a mediator of the relationship between personality and subjective well-being. Frontiers in Psychology, 4, 612.

Guilford, J.P. (1950). Creativity. American Psychologist, 5(9), 444-454.

Dahl, D. W., et al. (2003). How many ways can you say something? The preservation of ambiguity in an ambiguous context. Creativity Research Journal, 15(2-3), 147-157.

Roseth, C. J., et al. (2008). The impact of argumentation and problem-solving on learning and reasoning development in a middle school science classroom. Cognition and Instruction, 26(3), 365-397.

Schoenfeld, A. H. (1985). Mathematical problem solving. Academic Press.

Isaksen, S. G., & Gaulin, J. P. (2005). A reexamination of brainstorming research: Implications for research and practice. Gifted Child Quarterly, 49(4), 315-329.

Barron, B., et al. (1998). Doing with understanding: Lessons from research on problem- and project-based learning. Journal of the Learning Sciences, 7(3-4), 271-311.

Baird, B., et al. (2012). Inspired by Distraction: Mind Wandering Facilitates Creative Incubation. Psychological Science, 23(10), 1117-1122.

Sio, U. N., et al. (2013). Incubation and the resolution of fixation. Psychonomic Bulletin & Review, 20(4), 874-881.

Amabile, T. M., et al. (2002). Effects of external pressure on creative performance: An attributional perspective. Psychological Science, 13(4), 393-396.

Amabile, T. M. (1997). Motivating creativity in organizations: On doing what you love and loving what you do. Personality and Social Psychology Bulletin, 23(10), 1076-1087.

Paulus, P. B., & Yang, H. C. (2000). Idea generation in groups: A basis for creativity in organizations. Organizational Behavior and Human Decision Processes, 82(1), 76-87.

Hofmann, S. G., Asnaani, A., Vonk, I. J., Sawyer, A. T., & Fang, A. (2012). The Efficacy of Cognitive Behavioral Therapy: A Review of Meta-analyses. Cognitive Therapy and Research, 36(5), 427-440.

Lambert, M. J. (2013). The efficacy and effectiveness of psychotherapy. In M. J. Lambert (Ed.), Bergin and Garfield's Handbook of Psychotherapy and Behavior Change (6th ed., pp. 169-218). Wiley.

Cohen, S., & Wills, T. A. (1985). Stress, social support, and the buffering hypothesis. Psychological Bulletin, 98(2), 310-357.

Bolger, N., DeLongis, A., Kessler, R. C., & Schilling, E. A. (1989). Effects of daily stress on negative mood. Journal of Personality and Social Psychology, 57(5), 808-818.

Farb, N. A., Segal, Z. V., Mayberg, H., Bean, J., McKeon, D., Fatima, Z., & Anderson, A. K. (2007). Attending to the present: Mindfulness meditation reveals distinct neural modes of self-reference. Social Cognitive and Affective Neuroscience, 2(4), 313-322.

Hölzel, B. K., Lazar, S. W., Gard, T., Schuman-Olivier, Z., Vago, D. R., & Ott, U. (2011). How does mindfulness meditation work? Proposing mechanisms of action from a conceptual and neural perspective. Perspectives on Psychological Science, 6(6), 537-559.

Keng, S. L., Smoski, M. J., & Robins, C. J. (2013). Effects of mindfulness on psychological health: A review of empirical studies. Clinical Psychology Review, 31(6), 1041-1056.

Weng, H. Y., Fox, A. S., Shackman, A. J., Stodola, D. E., Caldwell, J. Z., Olson, M. C., ... & Davidson, R. J. (2013). Compassion training alters altruism and neural responses to suffering. Psychological Science, 24(7), 1171-1180.

Baikie, K. A., & Wilhelm, K. (2005). Emotional and physical health benefits of expressive writing. Advances in Psychiatric Treatment, 11(5), 338-346.

Pennebaker, J. W., & Beall, S. K. (1986). Confronting a traumatic event: Toward an understanding of inhibition and disease. Journal of Abnormal Psychology, 95(3), 274-281.

Klein, K., & Boals, A. (2001). Expressive writing can increase working memory capacity. Journal of Experimental Psychology: General, 130(3), 520-533.

Lepore, S. J., & Smyth, J. M. (2002). The writing cure: How expressive writing promotes health and emotional well-being. American Psychological Association.

Mayer, J. D., & Salovey, P. (1997). What is emotional intelligence? In P. Salovey & D. Sluyter (Eds.), Emotional development and emotional intelligence: Educational implications (pp. 3-31). Basic Books.

Paul, R., & Elder, L. (2006). Critical thinking: The nature of critical and creative thought. Journal of Developmental Education, 30(2), 34-35.

Bailin, S., Case, R., Coombs, J. R., & Daniels, L. B. (1999). Conceptualizing critical thinking. Journal of Curriculum Studies, 31(3), 285-302.

Linn, M. C., & Miller, L. M. (2018). Goal-based scenarios for learning and problem-solving. Routledge.

De Groot, A. D. (1965). Thought and choice in chess. Mouton.

Charness, N., Tuffiash, M., Krampe, R., Reingold, E., & Vasyukova, E. (2005). The role of deliberate practice in chess expertise. Applied Cognitive Psychology, 19(2), 151-165.

Willingham, D. T. (2007). Critical thinking: Why is it so hard to teach? American Educator, 31(2), 8-19.

Schmidt, H. G., Rotgans, J. I., & Yew, E. H. J. (2011). The process of problem-based learning: What works and why. Medical Education, 45(8), 792-806.

Paul, R., & Elder, L. (2006). Critical thinking: The nature of critical and creative thought. Journal of Developmental Education, 30(2), 34-35.

University of Reading. (2016). Pointer use aids reading comprehension. Retrieved from https://www.reading.ac.uk/news-and-events/releases/PR668641.aspx

Michael H. Connors, et al. (2019). Training in Speed of Processing, Working Memory, and Attentional Control. Psychonomic Bulletin & Review, 26(3), 878–894.

University of Washington. (2020). Active reading strategies can improve reading comprehension. Retrieved from https://www.washington.edu/news/2020/02/06/active-reading-strategies-can-improve-reading-comprehension/

Daniel L. Schwartz, et al. (2013). The ABCs of How We Learn: 26 Scientifically Proven Approaches, How They Work, and When to Use Them. Psychological Science, 24(9), 1760-1769.

Jaeggi, S. M., Buschkuehl, M., Jonides, J., & Perrig, W. J. (2008). Improving fluid intelligence with training on working memory. Proceedings of the National Academy of Sciences, 105(19), 6829-6833.

Mrazek, M. D., Franklin, M. S., Phillips, D. T., Baird, B., & Schooler, J. W. (2013). Mindfulness training improves working memory capacity and GRE performance while reducing mind wandering. Psychological Science, 24(5), 776-781.

Röer, J. P., Bell, R., & Buchner, A. (2013). Is the method of loci an efficient method for learning a structured list of face–name pairs? Memory & Cognition, 41(2), 309-319.

Taub, E., Uswatte, G., & Elbert, T. (2002). New treatments in neurorehabilitation founded on basic research. Nature Reviews Neuroscience, 3(3), 228-236.

Cicerone, K. D., Langenbahn, D. M., Braden, C., Malec, J. F., Kalmar, K., Fraas, M., ... & Ashman, T. (2011). Evidence-based cognitive rehabilitation: Updated review of the literature from 2003 through 2008. Archives of Physical Medicine and Rehabilitation, 92(4), 519-530.

Kivipelto, M., Ngandu, T., Laatikainen, T., Winblad, B., Soininen, H., & Tuomilehto, J. (2017). Risk score for the prediction of dementia risk in 20 years among middle-aged people: a longitudinal, population-based study. The Lancet Neurology, 16(11), 735-741.

Cornwell, B., Laumann, E. O., & Schumm, L. P. (2008). The social connectedness of older adults: A national profile. American Sociological Review, 73(2), 185-203.

Holt-Lunstad, J., Smith, T. B., & Layton, J. B. (2010). Social relationships and mortality risk: A meta-analytic review. PLOS Medicine, 7(7), e1000316.

Primack, B. A., Shensa, A., Sidani, J. E., Whaite, E. O., Lin, L. Y., Rosen, D., ... & Miller, E. (2017). Social media use and perceived social isolation among young adults in the US. PLOS ONE, 12(8), e0182143.

Musick, M. A., & Wilson, J. (2003). Volunteering and depression: The role of psychological and social resources in different age groups. Social Science & Medicine, 56(2), 259-269.

Reis, H. T., Collins, W. A., & Berscheid, E. (2000). The relationship context of human behavior and development. Psychological Bulletin, 126(6), 844-872.

Tang, Y. Y., et al. (2015). The neuroscience of mindfulness meditation. Nature Reviews Neuroscience, 16(4), 213-225.

Black, D. S., et al. (2013). Mindfulness meditation and improvement in sleep quality and daytime impairment among older adults with sleep disturbances: A randomized clinical trial. JAMA Internal Medicine, 173(4), 494-501.

Gothe, N. P., et al. (2013). Yoga enhances positive psychological states in young adult women. Journal of Alternative and Complementary Medicine, 19(11), 879-886.

Colcombe, S. J., et al. (2006). Aerobic fitness reduces brain tissue loss in aging humans. Journals of Gerontology Series A: Biological Sciences and Medical Sciences, 61(11), 1166-1170.

McEwen, B. S. (2016). Stress, adaptation, and disease: Allostasis and allostatic load. Annals of the New York Academy of Sciences, 840(1), 33-44.

Lupien, S. J., et al. (2009). Effects of stress throughout the lifespan on the brain, behaviour and cognition. Nature Reviews Neuroscience, 10(6), 434-445.

Mather, M., & Harley, C. W. (2016). The locus coeruleus: Essential for maintaining cognitive function and the aging brain. Trends in Cognitive Sciences, 20(3), 214-226.

Walker, M. P. (2009). The Role of Sleep in Cognition and Emotion. Annals of the New York Academy of Sciences, 1156(1), 168-197.

Lim, A. S. P., & Kowgier, M. (2013). Sleep Fragmentation and the Risk of Incident Alzheimer's Disease and Cognitive Decline in Older Persons. Sleep, 36(7), 1027-1032.

Irwin, M. R., & Vitiello, M. V. (2019). Implications of sleep disturbance and inflammation for Alzheimer's disease dementia. The Lancet Neurology, 18(3), 296-306.

Simons, D. J., Boot, W. R., Charness, N., Gathercole, S. E., Chabris, C. F., Hambrick, D. Z., & Stine-Morrow, E. A. (2016). Do "brain-training" programs work? Psychological Science in the Public Interest, 17(3), 103-186.

Valenzuela, M. J., & Sachdev, P. (2006). Brain reserve and dementia: a systematic review. Psychological Medicine, 36(4), 441-454.

Wilson, R. S., Scherr, P. A., Schneider, J. A., Tang, Y., & Bennett, D. A. (2007). Relation of cognitive activity to risk of developing Alzheimer disease. Neurology, 69(20), 1911-1920.

Pascual-Leone, A., Amedi, A., Fregni, F., & Merabet, L. B. (2005). The plastic human brain cortex. Annual Review of Neuroscience, 28, 377-401.

Hultsch, D. F., Hertzog, C., Small, B. J., & Dixon, R. A. (2003). Use it or lose it: engaged lifestyle as a buffer of cognitive decline in aging? Psychological Science, 14(3), 204-211.

Kuiper, J. S., Zuidersma, M., Oude Voshaar, R. C., Zuidema, S. U., van den Heuvel, E. R., & Stolk, R. P. (2015). Social relationships and risk of dementia: A systematic review and meta-analysis of longitudinal cohort studies. JAMA Psychiatry, 72(12), 1136-1142.

Borella, E., Carretti, B., Riboldi, F., & De Beni, R. (2010). Working memory training in older adults: evidence of transfer and maintenance effects. Psychology and Aging, 25(4), 767-778.

Hardy, J. L., Nelson, R. A., Thomason, M. E., & Sternberg, D. A. (2015). Enhancing cognitive abilities with comprehensive training: a large, online, randomized, active-controlled trial. PLOS ONE, 10(9), e0134467.

Mrazek, M. D., Franklin, M. S., Phillips, D. T., Baird, B., & Schooler, J. W. (2013). Mindfulness training improves working memory capacity and GRE performance while reducing mind wandering. Psychological Science, 24(5), 776-781.

Habibi, A., Cahn, B. R., Damasio, A., & Damasio, H. (2016). Neural correlates of accelerated auditory processing in children engaged in music training. Frontiers in Psychology, 7, 1263.

Abutalebi, J., & Green, D. W. (2012). Bilingualism tunes the anterior cingulate cortex for conflict monitoring. The Journal of Neuroscience, 32(14), 13435-13440.

Tolppanen, A. M., et al. (2012). Leisure-time physical activity from mid- to late life, body mass index, and risk of dementia. Neurology, 39(4), 504-512.

Voelcker-Rehage, C., & Niemann, C. (2013). Structural and functional brain changes related to different types of physical activity across the life span. Neuroscience & Biobehavioral Reviews, 37(9 Pt B), 2268-2295.

American Heart Association. (2022). Recommendations for Physical Activity in Adults and Kids. [https://www.heart.org/en/healthy-living/fitness/fitness-basics/aha-recs-for-physical-activity-in-adults]

Roig, M., et al. (2016). Resistance training enhances cognitive function in individuals with mild cognitive impairment. European Journal of Neuroscience, 44(12), 2645-2655.

Chang, Y. K., et al. (2018). Effects of resistance training on cognitive performance in older adults: a meta-analysis. Journal of Strength and Conditioning Research, 32(5), 1101-1107.

Chang, Y. K., et al. (2017). The effects of acute resistance exercise on attention and decision-making in older adults. Journal of Aging Research, 2017, 1-8.

Ludyga, S., et al. (2018). Effects of Aerobic Exercise on Cognitive Performance: Is It a Tempo Effect? Psychology of Sport and Exercise, 37, 128-134.

Hillman, C. H., et al. (2008). Be smart, exercise your heart: exercise effects on brain and cognition. Nature Reviews Neuroscience, 9(1), 58-65.

Birks, J. S., & Grimley Evans, J. (2009). Ginkgo biloba for cognitive impairment and dementia. Cochrane Database of Systematic Reviews, 1(1), CD003120.

Ng, T. P., Chiam, P. C., Lee, T., Chua, H. C., Lim, L., & Kua, E. H. (2006). Curry consumption and cognitive function in the elderly. American Journal of Epidemiology, 164(9), 898-906.

Glade, M. J., & Smith, K. (2015). Phosphatidylserine and the human brain. Nutrition, 31(6), 781-786.

Thal, L. J., Carta, A., Clarke, W. R., Ferris, S. H., & Friedland, R. P. (1996). Long-term oral physostigmine in Alzheimer's disease. Neurology, 47(1), 159-164.

Zhang, Y., Chen, J., Qiu, J., Li, Y., & Wang, J. (2017). Intakes of fish and polyunsaturated fatty acids and mild-to-severe cognitive impairment risks: A dose-response meta-analysis of 21 cohort studies. The American Journal of Clinical Nutrition, 105(1), 165-174.

Smith, A. D., Smith, S. M., de Jager, C. A., Whitbread, P., Johnston, C., Agacinski, G., ... & Refsum, H. (2010). Homocysteine-lowering by B vitamins slows the rate of accelerated brain atrophy in mild cognitive impairment: a randomized controlled trial. PLoS ONE, 5(9), e12244.

Littlejohns, T. J., Henley, W. E., Lang, I. A., Annweiler, C., Beauchet, O., Chaves, P. H., ... & Kestenbaum, B. R. (2014). Vitamin D and the risk of dementia and Alzheimer disease. Neurology, 83(10), 920-928.

Bowman, G. L., Dodge, H. H., Guyonnet, S., Zhou, N., Donohue, J. E., Zhu, H., ... & Frei, B. (2017). A blood-based nutritional risk index explains cognitive enhancement and decline in the multidomain Alzheimer prevention trial. Alzheimer's & Dementia, 13(7), 760-768.

Rao, S. S., & Adlard, P. A. (2020). Untangling the mechanisms underlying iron dyshomeostasis in Alzheimer's disease: A narrative review. Ageing Research Reviews, 59, 101043.

Scarmeas, N., Stern, Y., Tang, M. X., Mayeux, R., & Luchsinger, J. A. (2006). Mediterranean diet and risk for Alzheimer's disease. Annals of Neurology, 59(6), 912-921.

Morris, M. C., Tangney, C. C., Wang, Y., Sacks, F. M., Barnes, L. L., Bennett, D. A., & Aggarwal, N. T. (2015). MIND diet associated with reduced incidence of Alzheimer's disease. Alzheimer's & Dementia, 11(9), 1007-1014.

Oulhaj, A., Jernéré, N., Refsum, H., & Smith, A. D. (2016). de Jager, C. A. (2016). Omega-3 fatty acid status enhances the prevention of cognitive decline by B vitamins in mild cognitive impairment. Journal of Alzheimer's Disease, 50(2), 547-557.

Devore, E. E., Kang, J. H., Breteler, M. M., & Grodstein, F. (2012). Dietary intakes of berries and flavonoids in relation to cognitive decline. Annals of Neurology, 72(1), 135-143.

Chew, E. Y., Clemons, T. E., Agrón, E., Launer, L. J., Grodstein, F., & Bernstein, P. S. (2014). Effect of omega-3 fatty acids, lutein/zeaxanthin, or other nutrient supplementation on cognitive function: the AREDS2 randomized clinical trial. JAMA, 311(3), 267-277.

Grandjean, P. et al. (1997). Cognitive deficit in 7-year-old children with prenatal exposure to methylmercury. Neurotoxicology and Teratology, 19(6), 417-428.

Weiss, B. et al. (2004). Cognitive deficits at age 7 in children with prenatal exposure to methylmercury. Neurotoxicology and Teratology, 26(3), 359-371.

Shih, R. A. et al. (2006). Cumulative lead dose and cognitive function in adults: a review of studies that measured both blood lead and bone lead. Environmental Health Perspectives, 114(12), 1847-1854.

Evans, G. W. (2006). Child development and the physical environment. Annual Review of Psychology, 57, 423-451.

Lepore, S. J. et al. (2015). Noise and urban children: A review of recent research. Journal of the Acoustical Society of America, 137(6), 3476-3482.

Vohs, K. D. et al. (2013). Physical order produces healthy choices, generosity, and conventionality, whereas disorder produces creativity. Psychological Science, 24(9), 1860-1867.

Dadvand, P. et al. (2015). Green spaces and cognitive development in primary schoolchildren. Proceedings of the National Academy of Sciences, 112(26), 7937-7942.

Power, M. C. et al. (2016). The association of long-term exposure to particulate matter air pollution with brain MRI findings: the ARIC Study. Environmental Health Perspectives, 124(9), 1425-1433.

Chen, H. et al. (2017). Living near major roads and the incidence of dementia, Parkinson's disease, and multiple sclerosis: a population-based cohort study. The Lancet, 389(10070), 718-726.

Calderón-Garcidueñas, L. et al. (2015). Air pollution and children: neural and tight junction antibodies and combustion metals, the role of barrier breakdown and brain immunity in neurodegeneration. Journal of Alzheimer's Disease, 43(3), 1039-1058.

Clark, C. et al. (2012). A review of the epidemiological evidence concerning the reproductive health effects of exposure to PM(2.5) ambient air pollution. Environmental Research, 117, 180-191.

Grandjean, P. et al. (1997). Cognitive deficit in 7-year-old children with prenatal exposure to methylmercury. Neurotoxicology and Teratology, 19(6), 417-428.

Lanphear, B. P. et al. (2005). Cognitive deficits associated with blood lead concentrations <10 μg/dL in US children and adolescents. Public Health Reports, 120(3), 282-288.

Roses, A. D. (1996). Apolipoprotein E and Alzheimer's disease: a rapidly expanding field with medical and epidemiological consequences. Annals of the New York Academy of Sciences, 802(1), 50-57.

De Jager, P. L., & Bennett, D. A. (2013). An empirical aging and mortality model for use in epidemiologic studies of the elderly. In Neuroepidemiology (Vol. 40, No. 2, pp. 133-144). Karger Publishers.

Tan, M. S., Yu, J. T., & Tan, L. (2013). Bridging integrator 1 (BIN1): form, function, and Alzheimer's disease. Trends in molecular medicine, 19(10), 594-603.

Sniekers, S., Stringer, S., Watanabe, K., Jansen, P. R., Coleman, J. R., Krapohl, E., ... & Posthuma, D. (2017). Genome-wide association meta-analysis of 78,308 individuals identifies new loci and genes influencing human intelligence. Nature genetics, 49(7), 1107-1112.

Piaget, J. (1952). The origins of intelligence in children. International Universities Press.

Giedd, J. N., Blumenthal, J., Jeffries, N. O., Castellanos, F. X., Liu, H., Zijdenbos, A., ... & Rapoport, J. L. (1999). Brain development during childhood and adolescence: A longitudinal MRI study. Nature Neuroscience, 2(10), 861-863.

Salthouse, T. A. (2009). When does age-related cognitive decline begin? Neurobiology of Aging, 30(4), 507-514.

Stern, Y. (2012). Cognitive reserve in ageing and Alzheimer's disease. The Lancet Neurology, 11(11), 1006-1012.

Ferini-Strambi, L., Baietto, C., Di Gioia, M. R., Castaldi, P., Castronovo, C., Zucconi, M., ... & Cappa, S. F. (2003). Cognitive dysfunction in patients with obstructive sleep apnea (OSA): partial reversibility after continuous positive airway pressure (CPAP). Brain Research Bulletin, 61(1), 87-92.

Osorio, R. S., Gumb, T., Pirraglia, E., Varga, A. W., Lu, S. E., Lim, J., ... & Alzheimer's Disease Neuroimaging Initiative. (2015). Sleep-disordered breathing advances cognitive decline in the elderly. Neurology, 84(19), 1964-1971.

Yaffe, K., Laffan, A. M., Harrison, S. L., Redline, S., Spira, A. P., Ensrud, K. E., ... & Stone, K. L. (2011). Sleep-disordered breathing, hypoxia, and risk of mild cognitive impairment and dementia in older women. JAMA, 306(6), 613-619.

Kumar, A., & Haroon, E. (2016). Obesity and mood disorders: a shared pathophysiology. Psychiatric Times, 33(1), 17-20.

Gunstad, J., Paul, R. H., Cohen, R. A., Tate, D. F., Spitznagel, M. B., & Gordon, E. (2007). Elevated body mass index is associated with executive dysfunction in otherwise healthy adults. Comprehensive Psychiatry, 48(1), 57-61.

Smith, E., Hay, P., Campbell, L., & Trollor, J. N. (2011). A review of the association between obesity and cognitive function across the lifespan: implications for novel approaches to prevention and treatment. Obesity Reviews, 12(9), 740-755.

Iadecola, C., & Davisson, R. L. (2008). Hypertension and cerebrovascular dysfunction. Cell metabolism, 7(6), 476-484.

Qiu, C., Winblad, B., & Fratiglioni, L. (2005). The age-dependent relation of blood pressure to cognitive function and dementia. The Lancet Neurology, 4(8), 487-499.

Tzourio, C., Laurent, S., & Debette, S. (2014). Is hypertension associated with an accelerated aging of the brain? Hypertension, 63(5), 894-903.

Gorelick, P. B., Scuteri, A., Black, S. E., DeCarli, C., Greenberg, S. M., Iadecola, C., ... & Schneider, J. A. (2011). Vascular contributions to cognitive impairment and dementia: a statement for healthcare professionals from the American Heart Association/American Stroke Association. Stroke, 42(9), 2672-2713.

Ott, A., Breteler, M. M., de Bruyne, M. C., van Harskamp, F., Grobbee, D. E., & Hofman, A. (1997). Atrial fibrillation and dementia in a population-based study: the Rotterdam Study. Stroke, 28(2), 316-321.

Richardson, K., Schoen, M., French, B., Umscheid, C. A., Mitchell, M. D., Arnold, S. E., ... & Bravata, D. M. (2013). Statins and cognitive function: a systematic review. Annals of Internal Medicine, 159(10), 688-697.

Biessels, G. J., & Despa, F. (2018). Cognitive decline and dementia in diabetes mellitus: Mechanisms and clinical implications. Nature Reviews Endocrinology, 14(10), 591-604.

Qiu, C., Winblad, B., & Fratiglioni, L. (2005). The age-dependent relation of blood pressure to cognitive function and dementia. The Lancet Neurology, 4(8), 487-499.

Kanagasabai, T., Ardern, C. I., & Inflammation, B. (2015). Contribution of inflammation, oxidative stress, and antioxidants to the relationship between sleep duration and cardiometabolic health. Sleep, 38(12), 1905-1912.

McIntyre, R. S., & Cha, D. S. (2016). Cognitive deficits and functional outcomes in major depressive disorder: determinants, substrates, and treatment interventions. Depression and Anxiety, 33(9), 297-308.

Arnsten, A. F. (2009). Stress signalling pathways that impair prefrontal cortex structure and function. Nature Reviews Neuroscience, 10(6), 410-422.

Faraone, S. V., & Biederman, J. (2005). What is the prevalence of adult ADHD? Results of a population screen of 966 adults. Journal of Attention Disorders, 9(2), 384-391.

Robinson, L. J., Thompson, J. M., Gallagher, P., Goswami, U., Young, A. H., & Ferrier, I. N. (2006). A meta-analysis of cognitive deficits in euthymic patients with bipolar disorder. Journal of Affective Disorders, 93(1-3), 105-115.

Orr, H. T., & Zoghbi, H. Y. (2007). Trinucleotide repeat disorders. Annual Review of Neuroscience, 30, 575-621.

Geschwind, M. D. (2015). Prion diseases. Continuum: Lifelong Learning in Neurology, 21(6), 1612-1638.

Sullivan, E. V., & Pfefferbaum, A. (2009). Neuroimaging of the Wernicke-Korsakoff syndrome. Alcohol and Alcoholism, 44(2), 155-165.

Armstrong, M. J., & Litvan, I. (2015). A guide to the management of PSP: Part 2. Neurodegenerative Diseases Management, 5(3), 237-248.

Aarsland, D., Kurz, M. W., & Beyer, M. K. (2008). Dementia in Parkinson's disease. Current Opinion in Neurology, 21(6), 676-682.

Iadecola, C. (2013). The pathobiology of vascular dementia. Neuron, 80(4), 844-866.

Rascovsky, K., Hodges, J. R., Knopman, D., Mendez, M. F., Kramer, J. H., et al. (2011). Sensitivity of revised diagnostic criteria for the behavioural variant of frontotemporal dementia. Brain, 134(9), 2456-2477.

McKeith, I. G., Dickson, D. W., Lowe, J., Emre, M., O'Brien, J. T., et al. (2005). Diagnosis and management of dementia with Lewy bodies: third report of the DLB Consortium. Neurology, 65(12), 1863-1872.

Alzheimer, A. (1907). Über eine eigenartige Erkrankung der Hirnrinde. Allgemeine Zeitschrift für Psychiatrie und Psychisch-Gerichtliche Medizin, 64, 146–148.

Hardy, J., & Selkoe, D. J. (2002). The amyloid hypothesis of Alzheimer's disease: progress and problems on the road to therapeutics. Science, 297(5580), 353–356.

Sperling, R. A., Aisen, P. S., Beckett, L. A., et al. (2011). Toward defining the preclinical stages of Alzheimer's disease: Recommendations from the National Institute on Aging-Alzheimer's Association workgroups on diagnostic guidelines for Alzheimer's disease. Alzheimer's & Dementia, 7(3), 280–292.

Cummings, J. L., Morstorf, T., & Zhong, K. (2014). Alzheimer's disease drug-development pipeline: few candidates, frequent failures. Alzheimer's Research & Therapy, 6(4), 37.

Squire, L. R. (2009). Memory and brain systems: 1969-2009. Journal of Neuroscience, 29(41), 12711-12716.

Erickson, K. I., et al. (2011). Exercise training increases size of hippocampus and improves memory. Proceedings of the National Academy of Sciences, 108(7), 3017-3022.

Zeidan, F., et al. (2010). Mindfulness meditation improves cognition: Evidence of brief mental training. Consciousness and Cognition, 19(2), 597-605.

Goleman, D. (1995). Emotional Intelligence: Why It Can Matter More Than IQ. Bantam Books.

Carlson, N. R. (2016). Physiology of Behavior. Pearson.

Kandel, E. R., Schwartz, J. H., & Jessell, T. M. (2000). Principles of Neural Science (4th ed.). McGraw-Hill.

www.ingramcontent.com/pod-product-compliance
Lightning Source LLC
Chambersburg PA
CBHW052151110526
44591CB00012B/1942